OPPOSING
VIEWPOINTS®
SERIES

The U.S. Intelligence Community

Other Books of Related Interest:

Opposing Viewpoints Series

Presidential Powers

Terrorism

War Crimes

At Issue Series

Are Privacy Rights Violated?

Homeland Security

Is Torture Ever Justified?

Current Controversies Series

Afghanistan

Domestic Wiretapping

"Congress shall make no law ... abridging the freedom of speech, or of the press."

First Amendment to the U.S. Constitution

The basic foundation of our democracy is the First Amendment guarantee of freedom of expression. The Opposing Viewpoints Series is dedicated to the concept of this basic freedom and the idea that it is more important to practice it than to enshrine it.

OPPOSING
VIEWPOINTS®
SERIES

The U.S. Intelligence Community

Noah Berlatsky, Book Editor

GREENHAVEN PRESS
A part of Gale, Cengage Learning

GALE
CENGAGE Learning™

Detroit • New York • San Francisco • New Haven, Conn • Waterville, Maine • London

Christine Nasso, *Publisher*
Elizabeth Des Chenes, *Managing Editor*

© 2011 Greenhaven Press, a part of Gale, Cengage Learning

Gale and Greenhaven Press are registered trademarks used herein under license.

For more information, contact:
Greenhaven Press
27500 Drake Rd.
Farmington Hills, MI 48331-3535
Or you can visit our Internet site at gale.cengage.com

Articles in Greenhaven Press anthologies are often edited for length to meet page require-ments. In addition, original titles of these works are changed to clearly present the main thesis and to explicitly indicate the author's opinion. Every effort is made to ensure that Greenhaven Press accurately reflects the original intent of the authors. Every effort has been made to trace the owners of copyrighted material.

Cover image courtesy of Jeff Bane, CMB Design Partners.

LIBRARY OF CONGRESS CATALOGING-IN-PUBLICATION DATA

The U.S. intelligence community / Noah Berlatsky, book editor.
    p. cm. -- (Opposing viewpoints)
    Includes bibliographical references and index.
    ISBN 978-0-7377-5245-8 (hardcover) -- ISBN 978-0-7377-5246-5 (pbk.)
    1. Intelligence service--United States--Juvenile literature. I. Berlatsky, Noah.
    JK468.I6U2 2011
    327.1273--dc22

                                                                2010033440

Printed in the United States of America
1 2 3 4 5 6 7 15 14 13 12 11

Contents

Chapter 3: What Impact Does the U.S. Intelligence Community Have on Foreign Affairs?

Chapter 4: What Role Should Torture Play in U.S. Intelligence?

Why Consider Opposing Viewpoints?

> *"The only way in which a human being can make some approach to knowing the whole of a subject is by hearing what can be said about it by persons of every variety of opinion and studying all modes in which it can be looked at by every character of mind. No wise man ever acquired his wisdom in any mode but this."*
>
> John Stuart Mill

In our media-intensive culture it is not difficult to find differing opinions. Thousands of newspapers and magazines and dozens of radio and television talk shows resound with differing points of view. The difficulty lies in deciding which opinion to agree with and which "experts" seem the most credible. The more inundated we become with differing opinions and claims, the more essential it is to hone critical reading and thinking skills to evaluate these ideas. Opposing Viewpoints books address this problem directly by presenting stimulating debates that can be used to enhance and teach these skills. The varied opinions contained in each book examine many different aspects of a single issue. While examining these conveniently edited opposing views, readers can develop critical thinking skills such as the ability to compare and contrast authors' credibility, facts, argumentation styles, use of persuasive techniques, and other stylistic tools. In short, the Opposing Viewpoints Series is an ideal way to attain the higher-level thinking and reading skills so essential in a culture of diverse and contradictory opinions.

In addition to providing a tool for critical thinking, Opposing Viewpoints books challenge readers to question their own strongly held opinions and assumptions. Most people form their opinions on the basis of upbringing, peer pressure, and personal, cultural, or professional bias. By reading carefully balanced opposing views, readers must directly confront new ideas as well as the opinions of those with whom they disagree. This is not to simplistically argue that everyone who reads opposing views will—or should—change his or her opinion. Instead, the series enhances readers' understanding of their own views by encouraging confrontation with opposing ideas. Careful examination of others' views can lead to the readers' understanding of the logical inconsistencies in their own opinions, perspective on why they hold an opinion, and the consideration of the possibility that their opinion requires further evaluation.

Evaluating Other Opinions

To ensure that this type of examination occurs, Opposing Viewpoints books present all types of opinions. Prominent spokespeople on different sides of each issue as well as well-known professionals from many disciplines challenge the reader. An additional goal of the series is to provide a forum for other, less known, or even unpopular viewpoints. The opinion of an ordinary person who has had to make the decision to cut off life support from a terminally ill relative, for example, may be just as valuable and provide just as much insight as a medical ethicist's professional opinion. The editors have two additional purposes in including these less known views. One, the editors encourage readers to respect others' opinions—even when not enhanced by professional credibility. It is only by reading or listening to and objectively evaluating others' ideas that one can determine whether they are worthy of consideration. Two, the inclusion of such viewpoints encourages the important critical thinking skill of objectively evaluating an author's credentials and bias. This evaluation will illuminate an author's reasons for taking a particular stance on an issue and will aid in readers' evaluation of the author's ideas.

It is our hope that these books will give readers a deeper understanding of the issues debated and an appreciation of the complexity of even seemingly simple issues when good and honest people disagree. This awareness is particularly important in a democratic society such as ours in which people enter into public debate to determine the common good. Those with whom one disagrees should not be regarded as enemies but rather as people whose views deserve careful examination and may shed light on one's own.

Thomas Jefferson once said that "difference of opinion leads to inquiry, and inquiry to truth." Jefferson, a broadly educated man, argued that "if a nation expects to be ignorant and free . . . it expects what never was and never will be." As individuals and as a nation, it is imperative that we consider the opinions of others and examine them with skill and discernment. The Opposing Viewpoints Series is intended to help readers achieve this goal.

David L. Bender and Bruno Leone,
Founders

Introduction

> "We need to design a balanced strategy for the long haul, to attack terrorists and prevent their ranks from swelling while at the same time protecting our country against future attacks.... The massive departments and agencies that prevailed in the great struggles of the twentieth century must work together in new ways, so that all the instruments of national power can be combined."
>
> —The 9/11 Commission Report, July 2004

On September 11, 2001, terrorists seized control of four commercial airliners in the United States. One plane was flown into the Pentagon, one crash-landed in Pennsylvania, and two flew into the World Trade Center in New York, destroying the buildings. Including the nineteen hijackers, 2,995 people died in the attacks. This was the worst terrorist attack on American soil in history. Responding to the events, President George W. Bush said in an address to the nation on the evening of September 11, "Thousands of lives were suddenly ended by evil, despicable acts of terror.... The search is underway for those who are behind these evil acts."

Many people argued that the attacks could have been prevented by better U.S. intelligence efforts. Perhaps the most high-profile criticism came from the bipartisan 9/11 Commission created by Congress and chaired by former New Jersey governor Thomas Kean. The commission report, released in 2004, said that "U.S. intelligence gathering was fragmented and poorly coordinated" before the attacks, according to a 2004 article on CNN.com. In particular, the report singled out

Central Intelligence Agency (CIA) director George Tenet for failing to develop a strategy to combat terrorism before the attack. The commission also "found that the intelligence community suffered from a lack of institutional imagination," according to Joshua Rovner and Austin Long, writing in *Breakthroughs* in 2005. "This," Rovner and Long stated, "made it impossible for most analysts and policymakers to accurately gauge the terrorist threat."

Commentators also suggested that policy makers had failed to act upon information provided to them by intelligence agencies. For example, President George W. Bush "had been warned by American intelligence agencies in early August [2001] that Osama bin Laden [leader of the terrorist organization al Qaeda, which had coordinated the attacks,] was seeking to hijack aircraft," according to David E. Sanger in a 2002 *New York Times* article. The White House said it did not realize the planes would be flown into buildings; however, there is some evidence that a scenario in which terrorists used planes as missiles may at least have been contemplated before 9/11. For example, the North Atlantic Treaty Organization (NATO) conducted simulations in which hijacked airplanes were flown into various buildings. "One of the imagined targets was the World Trade Center," according to Steven Komarow and Tom Squitieri in a 2004 article in *USA Today*.

The magnitude of the 9/11 attacks, and the revelations of both intelligence and policy failures, have led to many conspiracy theories. Most of these theories suggest that 9/11 may have been an intelligence operation carried out by the U.S. government itself. For example, a popular conspiracy theory suggests that the World Trade Center (WTC) was destroyed not by planes hitting the buildings, but by a controlled demolition. This has been deemed impossible, however, because "demolition professionals always blow the bottom floors of a structure first, but the WTC tower collapses began at the upper levels, where the planes hit the buildings," according to a

2009 article on America.gov. The magazine *Popular Mechanics* also featured an extensive article in 2005 that debunked sixteen popular conspiracy theories, concluding that "a few theories are based on something as innocent as a reporting error on that chaotic day" while "others are the byproducts of cynical imaginations that aim to inject suspicion and animosity into the public debate."

Some commentators have argued that 9/11 was not really caused by intelligence failures at all. For example, in a 2008 *Washington Post* article, Mark M. Lowenthal argued that "no one has yet revealed the one or two or 10 things that, had they been done differently, might have prevented the attacks. . . . Even if every 'dot' had been connected, they would not have led to the critical intelligence needed to stop those four planes on that Tuesday morning." Lowenthal contends that intelligence should not be expected to predict big, surprising events, but instead should keep "policymakers generally well-informed on a recurring basis so that they can make decisions with a reasonable sense of confidence." Lowenthal concludes that the emphasis on prediction undermines the real use of intelligence and gives people a false sense of security.

The present volume examines other intelligence issues and challenges that have arisen in the years since 9/11, in chapters focusing on these questions: Is the U.S. Intelligence Community Working Effectively? Does the U.S. Intelligence Community Advance Domestic Security? What Impact Does the U.S. Intelligence Community Have on Foreign Affairs? and What Role Should Torture Play in U.S. Intelligence? The different viewpoints debate what the U.S. intelligence community should do, how it should be organized, and how well or how poorly it is doing its job.

OPPOSING
VIEWPOINTS®
SERIES

CHAPTER 1

Is the U.S. Intelligence Community Working Effectively?

Chapter Preface

Following the September 11, 2001, terrorist attacks in which commercial airliners were flown into the World Trade Center and the Pentagon, a number of changes were made to airport security. In particular, "knives and cutting instruments of any size, made of metal, plastic or any other material," were banned from all flights, according to Paul Zielbauer and John Sullivan in the *New York Times* on September 13, 2001. Curbside check-in was also eliminated, and passenger planes ceased carrying cargo or mail to reduce the risk of bombs.

In subsequent years, further restrictions were placed on air travel in response to terrorist attempts or terrorist threats. For example, in December 2001, a terrorist on an international flight attempted to detonate a bomb in his shoe. After receiving threats of other possible shoe bombings, federal officials responded "by urging airport passengers to remove shoes at security checkpoints," according to Alan Gathright in a 2003 *San Francisco Chronicle* article. Similarly, threats that terrorists might carry liquid explosives onto planes surfaced in 2006. This caused airlines to place limits on the amount of liquids and gels that passengers could carry onto flights. President George W. Bush, speaking about the new restrictions on liquids said that "the inconvenience . . . occurs because we will take the steps necessary to protect the American people," as quoted in a 2006 article on CNET News.

Not all commentators have been impressed with the new security restrictions, however. For example, Bruce Schneier, a critic of the Transportation Safety Administration's efforts, argues that "counter-terrorism in the airport is a show designed to make people feel better. . . . Only two things have made flying safer: the reinforcement of cockpit doors, and the fact that passengers know now to resist hijackers," as quoted in a 2008 article in the *Atlantic Monthly*. Schneier further claims that the post-9/11 security measures make airports no safer, and that the United States would do better to spend its resources on "intelligence, investigations, and emergency response."

Compounding airlines' problems is the difficulty of providing airport security with useful intelligence information. "Airport operators have long felt that timely information and intelligence sharing could help them in their handling of security operations. Proactive security managers realize the importance of preparedness: information outlining threats to airports can help reduce risk. However, most managers are constrained by their inability to access accurate, systematically collected, and processed information and by staffing limitations. Little, if any, information or intelligence is airport-specific and information that is broader in scope is seldom useful," according to Robert R. Raffell in a 2007 article on the Central Intelligence Agency's website.

Thus, how to organize airport security to best prevent terrorism remains a major problem for airlines, the government, and the intelligence community. The following viewpoints debate other bureaucratic and organizational challenges facing U.S. intelligence, as well as some possible solutions.

> *"The [director of national intelligence] can help solve the problems of the [intelligence community], but the office will need more authority, both legislatively and administratively."*

The Director of National Intelligence Improves Collaboration Between Agencies

Heinisha S. Jacques

Heinisha S. Jacques is a Defense Department intelligence employee. *In the following viewpoint, he argues that the U.S. intelligence agencies have historically had problems coordinating and working together. The attacks of September 11, 2001, helped remove some communications barriers, Jacques contends, and the office of the director of national intelligence (DNI) was created to support that change. Jacques concludes that the DNI should be able to facilitate better interagency communication, though additional authority would enhance those efforts.*

Heinisha S. Jacques, "Director of National Intelligence: Another Bureaucratic Layer or an Effective Office?" *DTIC Online*, December 2006. Reproduced by permission of the author.

As you read, consider the following questions:

1. What does Jacques say is one of the best examples of compartmentalization between intelligence agencies?
2. The findings of what commission led to the creation of the DNI, according to the author?
3. Since the DNI does not have sufficient authority, what will he or she have to rely on in order to address intelligence community problems, according to Jacques?

Since its inception, the intelligence community (IC) has had several persistent problems in the past that continue today. Three problems that are prevalent are information sharing, activity coordination, and validity of analysis. There have been "walls" within military and civilian intelligence organizations since World War I. These artificial barriers were used to compartmentalize information between emerging intelligence organizations. One of the best examples of compartmentalization occurred between the Federal Bureau of Investigation (FBI) and the Central Intelligence Agency (CIA). It was expected that the CIA would not share its intelligence with any other agency. The FBI did not want to share its information because of law enforcement sensitivities. As an intelligence employee of the Department of Defense, my personal observation is that the Naval Criminal and Investigative Service (NCIS) and Air Force Office of Special Investigations (AFOSI) are not seen as "real" counterintelligence organizations by Army counterintelligence professionals.

Agencies at Odds

During World War II, US Army Military Intelligence (MI), the Office of Naval Intelligence (ONI), and the FBI were at odds about their respective responsibilities. The FBI believed they were responsible for all domestic intelligence. The ONI believed it was responsible for internal security and domestic counterintelligence. As a result of this conflict, the intelligence organizations were reluctant to share intelligence. President Franklin Roosevelt hired an old and trusted friend, William "Wild Bill" Donovan to review the nation's intelligence. Donovan suggested that Roosevelt create a central agency to collate information and report significant issues to the President. Thus, the Office of the Coordinator of Information (COI) was created on July 11, 1941. Donovan was appointed to lead the COI, which had a staff of 600 and a budget of $10 million. Although COI was helping in reducing redundancies, it did not have the Army or Navy intelligence, or the FBI because they all feared COI would take over their current duties. COI was eventually dissolved October 1, 1945. The Central Intelligence Group (CIG) followed in 1947, then it became the CIA with the National Security Act of 1947.

Around the time the CIA was established, President [Harry] Truman created the Director of Central Intelligence (DCI). After the dissolution of COI, its various intelligence functions were divided between the State Department and the military services. Truman quickly realized the necessity for a centralized organization to oversee all intelligence; thus, the creation of the DCI. The National Security Act of 1947 determined the duties of the DCI, who was to be the head of the U.S. IC, act as the principal advisor to the President, and serve as the head of the CIA. Over the years, concern grew that the DCI was more focused on the CIA, than other organizations in the IC. Additionally, many believed having one person for both positions was overwhelming. As stated by Senator [Dianne] Feinstein in 2002, "The demands of these two full time jobs on the time and attention of any person, no matter how skilled in management, are overwhelming . . . Even if one person could handle both jobs . . . there would remain the perception that he or she is favoring either the community or the Agency."

September 11, 2001

On 11 September 2001, terrorists attacked the United States. Four planes were hijacked; two hitting the World Trade Center in New York, one hitting the Pentagon in Virginia, and a fourth, possibly heading for the White House, crashed in Pennsylvania. Approximately 3,000 people died in the attacks. In his address to the nation, President [George W.] Bush said:

> The search is underway for those who are behind these evil acts. I've directed the full resources of our intelligence and law enforcement communities to find those responsible and to bring them to justice. We will make no distinction between the terrorists who committed these acts and those who harbor them.

After the events of September 11th, walls within the IC came down, to some extent. The nation's leadership recognized the need to eliminate or reduce the "walls" which were now identified as obstructing the flow of intelligence. However, problems remained that can and have sometimes led to failed operations or an incomplete picture of certain situations. As a result of September 11th, the IC was closely scrutinized. The National Commission on Terrorist Attacks Upon the United States, known as the 9/11 Commission, investigated the failures of the IC. The findings of the 9/11 Commission led to the Intelligence Reform and Terrorism Prevention Act of 2004 (hereafter cited as the Intelligence Reform Act, PL 108-458) creating a Director of National Intelligence to serve as the "principal intelligence adviser to the President, and oversee and direct the acquisition of major collections systems."

Activities of intelligence communities have been limited in dissemination and coordination. Analysts are often required to coordinate their products before having them published. Depending on the product, analysts will have to coordinate with external agencies. It is not uncommon to receive a nonconcurrence from other agencies or even internally. While a nonconcurrence does not necessarily preclude an analyst from publishing a product, it can take away from the credibility of the product. Frustration often sets in, which often leads to untimely, inaccurate or "nonactionable" information.

Obstacles and Resource Shortages

Similar to information sharing, there are barriers in the world of intelligence operations, which prevent coordination. Some confuse the term coordination with the term permission. Coordination does not imply obtaining approval. Rather, it is a way of letting agencies or services that perform similar operations know what their sister agencies are doing and to receive feedback. However, avoiding surprises is paramount. In the operational world, coordination normally does not occur because of the sensitivity of operations. There is always concern that too many people will be involved in an operation, possibly ruining it. Coordination is now viewed as essential, but the culture has to change—or there should be the elimination of one or more redundant agencies.

Coincident with these problems, intelligence organizations are facing a mini crisis of personnel. Some are losing senior people to retirement, who will be difficult to replace. Thus began a mass recruiting and hiring effort. While most agencies were able to replenish, there was a companion problem—lack of experience. Although the newcomers were college graduates usually with a background in some regional study, they were new to intelligence analysis. Some new hires were placed in positions with little or no training until months later. While bringing a new perspective is positive, analysts' work would often be questioned due to their inexperience in intelligence. The second problem that often slowed the process with personnel, particularly for military intelligence, is a shortage. They do not have enough intelligence officers. With the onset

Intelligence Has Improved

Five years after 9/11 the question many have on their mind is whether our nation's Intelligence Community is better prepared to keep America safe? My answer to this question is yes and here is why. First, we understand and are better aligned to meet the terrorist threat, and second, we are sharing information better, thus increasing our opportunities to thwart terrorist operations.

I won't claim that we have, over the past five years, perfected the art of counterterrorism. What we have done, as illustrated by some of our successes, is vastly improve the Intelligence Community's ability to understand, and disrupt, organizations like al-Qa'ida [terrorist organization responsible for the September 11, 2001, attacks]. For example we have several times as many "all source" analysts focusing on the terrorist threat than were in place on 9/11. We also have devoted a great deal more resources to increasing our human intelligence collection. This is real, tangible progress. It represents better collection, better analysis, and better support for our leaders, which will lead to an increased understanding of how to combat our terrorist foes. And everyone has had a hand in these successes, from the DIA [Defense Intelligence Agency] to the NSA [National Security Agency] to the CIA [Central Intelligence Agency], to the FBI [Federal Bureau of Investigation], and of course to the [military] service intelligence entities.

John D. Negroponte, Director of National Intelligence website, September 7, 2006. www.dni.gov.

of Operation Iraqi Freedom[1] and Operation Enduring Freedom,[2] there was an increase in requests for intelligence officers. As demand increased, supply declined.

The 9/11 Commission's recommendation—the establishment of a cabinet level DNI [Director of National Intelligence]—if followed, was to be the solution to some problems plaguing the IC. While creating a non-biased director who could equally focus on all members of the IC seems like a panacea, this research will examine the current status of the DNI in its role to accomplish the legislative intent of the Intelligence Reform Act and determine what solutions it can bring to the existing shortfalls of the IC. It has not been uncommon, in United States history, to create new offices to solve problems (i.e., Department of Homeland Security[3] after September 11th). While the new offices may look good in organizational chart graphics, that sometimes can be the only "change." Eventually, the excitement wears off and one is left with another bureaucratic layer that has not solved any existing problems. Will the DNI be this type of office? . . .

The DNI Must Rely on Relationships

Is the Director of National Intelligence able to solve the persisting problems of the IC as required by the Intelligence and Reform Act? After conducting the analysis of competing hypotheses, the most likely hypothesis was that the DNI can help solve the problems of the IC, but the office will need more authority, both legislatively and administratively. . . .

The DNI will not likely receive additional authorities. Therefore, the ability of the DNI to solve the problems of the IC will partly depend on relationships. The DNI needs to

1. Operation Iraqi Freedom was the name given to the 2003 invasion of Iraq by U.S. forces

2. Operation Enduring Freedom was the name given to the 2001 invasion of Afghanistan by U.S. forces.

3. Created in 2001, the Department of Homeland Security is a cabinet-level office charged with protecting U.S. territory.

forge a cooperative working relationship with the heads of the various intelligence organizations within the IC. In areas where the DNI does not have authority, he will have to rely on good working relationships to help reach agreements or ensure compliance with policies. One example of important relationships is with the CIA. There were a number of media reports indicating the CIA initially had some trouble adjusting to the Office of the DNI. This was because the DCI [Director of Central Intelligence], also the director of the CIA, was dissolved, which decreased some functions of the CIA. Certain routines and products for which the CIA was responsible, such as briefing the president daily, were taken over by the DNI; reportedly a major cause of the rift between the two agencies. Once [General Michael] Hayden was confirmed as the new director of the CIA [in 2005], the outlook on its relationship with the DNI changed. . . . Hayden had a great working relationship already established with Ambassador John D. Negroponte [Director of National Intelligence 2005–2007]. Several senior intelligence officials believe this positive relationship will help foster better ties between the CIA and the DNI. . . .

This study [has] demonstrated that a number of factors affect the ability of the DNI to solve the problems of the IC. Solving or at least mitigating these problems will increase in complexity and difficulty over time. Additional authority would in all probability eventually improve the DNI. However, until those authorities are in place, the DNI can and should insist on inter- and intra-agency coordination through cooperative programs and make the creation of positive working relationships a management priority. [As Director of National Intelligence John D. Negroponte said in 2006:]

> So, yes, we do face a daunting set of challenges in today's world, and they are different challenges from those of the last century . . . There are ways in which we can maintain and extend important advantages, however, if we act with a

sense of urgency and if we embrace the imperatives and inevitability of change.

> *"It was the responsibility of the ODNI [Office of the Director of National Intelligence] to resolve all these problems—but the creation of the ODNI has apparently only intensified the fragmentation."*

The Director of National Intelligence Aggravates Agency Turf Wars

C. Boyden Gray

C. Boyden Gray is a former U.S. ambassador to the European Union. In the following viewpoint, he argues that a 2009 attempted airplane bombing demonstrates that the U.S. intelligence community continues to be divided by bureaucratic turf wars that interfere with intelligence sharing. Gray contends that the Office of the Director of National Intelligence has only worsened the turf wars by adding more bureaucracy. He concludes that the White House needs to demand better cooperation among intelligence agencies if it is to protect the American public.

C. Boyden Gray, "Gray: Turf War Hampers War on Terrorism," *Washington Times*, January 21, 2010. Copyright 2009 The Washington Times, LLC. Reproduced by permission.

As you read, consider the following questions:

1. According to Gray, what did the ODNI inspector general conclude about data integration in the intelligence community?

2. What does the author say that Congress and the White House should have done after 9/11 rather than creating the ODNI?

3. What did the chairman of the House Science and Technology Commmittee characterize as a "colossal failure," according to Gray?

The media focus on the criminal indictment and Mirandization of the Detroit bombing suspect has raised an important point but obscured an even more critical one related to the war on terrorism. The suspected bomber should clearly have been held for more questioning. But more important is what the unseemly rush to indictment tells us about the overall, fundamental systemic failure that occurred.

What we see is a continued, persistent "turf war" culture that divides prosecuting agencies like the Department of Justice and the FBI on the one hand and the intelligence agencies such as the National Security Agency, the CIA, and the Office of the Director of National Intelligence (ODNI) on the other—a divide that seems to have been aggravated by the creation of the ODNI and that resulted in the failure to screen the suspected bomber in the first place and then forfeited a treasure of intelligence from him about Yemen.

Even the most cursory review of the recent record will concern anyone worried about terrorism. Compare, for example, the bland report just released by the White House that all of the bureaucratic turf behavior and other barriers to information sharing that led to 9/11 have now "8 years later, largely been overcome," with the blistering report issued just a year ago by the ODNI inspector general that data integration across the intelligence community (IC) has been a total failure.

The IG found, for example, that IC information systems are "largely disconnected and incompatible" and lacking any "standard architecture supporting the storage and retrieval of sensitive intelligence." Moreover, found the IG, the "culture of protecting 'turf' remains a problem, and there are few if any consequences for failure to collaborate."

More specifically, the IG concluded that "there is no overall IC strategy or leadership structure to drive collaboration among national intelligence agency and law enforcement organizations." Here the IG also found that FBI collaboration with the IC is "hampered by frequent turnover within FBI senior ranks and by outdated IT systems."

Bearing in mind that the FBI manages the Terrorism Screening Center (TSC) and the watch lists, it is even more disturbing then to read the Justice Department's inspector general's report of just a few weeks ago that said the information system of the FBI is "severely outdated, cumbersome to use, and does not facilitate the searching and sharing of information."

It was the responsibility of the ODNI to resolve all of these problems—but the creation of the ODNI has apparently only intensified the fragmentation. As the IG found, its review revealed that even within the ODNI "poor collaboration has resulted in 'turf battles' among some of the ODNI offices, causing information and activities to be 'stove piped.'"

Congress and the White House would have been better served after 9/11 to put a whip-cracking entity in the Executive Office of the President to beat the intelligence and prosecuting teams together rather than create another layer of competing agencies.

Technology Systems Failing

The [Investigations and Oversight] Subcommittee [of the Committee on Science and Technology of the U.S. House of Representatives] has learned that the TIDE [Terrorist Identities Datamart Environment] database is suffering from serious, long-standing technical problems. The Subcommittee has also learned that a critical NCTC [National Counterterrorism Center] initiative, named "Railhead," which is intended to replace TIDE with enhanced capabilities has suffered from severe technical troubles, poor contractor management and weak government oversight. As a result, potentially hundreds of millions of dollars have been wasted, delivery schedules have slipped, contractor employees have been laid off in order to restrain escalating costs, and the NCTC is now scrambling either to fix the technical troubles or possibly to abandon the program altogether. The end result is a current IT [information technology] system used to identify terrorist threats that has been crippled by technical flaws and a new system that if actually deployed will leave our country more vulnerable than the existing yet flawed system in operation today.

Brad Miller, U.S. House of Representatives
Committee on Science and
Technology website, August 21, 2008.
http://democrats.science.house.gov.

As a result, there is little coherence in the contradictory White House conclusions that (1) "information sharing does not appear to have contributed to this intelligence failure" because no one was "prevented" from accessing information but that (2) "information technology within the CT community did not sufficiently enable the correlation of data that would have enabled analysts to highlight the relevant threat information." That is to say, no one was "prevented" from accessing relevant information, but no one was "enabled" to do it either.

The ODNI inspector general's report followed an Aug. 21, 2008, investigation request from the chairman of the investigations and oversight subcommittee of the House Science and Technology Committee. That request asked for an examination of what the chairman described as the ODNI's "colossal failure" to update the ODNI's terrorist intelligence database that provides the backbone of the FBI's consolidated terrorist watch list.

Bridging the intelligence/prosecution divide, as urged more than a year ago by the ODNI inspector general, is obviously a difficult task, just as it was before 9/11. But the way forward is not to remove the inspector general just after he describes the divide, along with the related incompetence of both the ODNI and FBI.

Maybe the key to a solution is to ask first why the inspector general was fired and replaced with a Justice Department employee who appears to have done nothing in the year following to modernize the FBI's information sharing in response to the IG's criticism. The problem goes beyond trying to track just one terrorist; it fundamentally jeopardizes the government's basic ability to grasp fully any of the threats it faces.

Who and what are they covering up? No doubt the congressional Armed Services, Intelligence, Homeland Security and Judiciary committees all think their own agency is in charge. But there is only one White House, and it will have to provide the missing coordination between the intelligence and law enforcement communities. Otherwise, each will continue to go its own way—prosecuting criminals on the one hand and fighting terrorists on the other—without truly collaborating to reduce risks to the public.

> *"Since its creation in 2003, the depart-
> ment [of Homeland Security] has done
> little to provide genuine security and
> much to encourage a pernicious politics
> of fear. We'd be better off without it."*

The Department of Homeland Security Should Be Abolished

Gene Healy

Gene Healy is a columnist for the Washington Examiner, *president at the Cato Institute, and the author of* The Cult of the Presidency. *In the following viewpoint, he argues that the Department of Homeland Security (DHS) was designed more because of political popularity than because it actually improves security. In addition, he claims that the DHS is wasteful and that it encourages programs that abridge individual liberty. He concludes that the department should be abolished.*

As you read, consider the following questions:

1. According to Healy, why did Tom Ridge conclude that he needed to resign as head of the Department of Homeland Security?

2. A congressional investigation in 2008 documented how much in failed DHS contracts, according to the author?

Gene Healy, "Abolish the DHS," *Washington Examiner*, August 25, 2009. Copyright © 2009 The Washington Newspaper Publishing Company. Reproduced by permission.

3. Why does Healy say that government would not become much smaller even if DHS were eliminated?

Does "time with my family" ever actually mean "time with my family" in Washington? Tom Ridge gave the standard resignation line when he stepped down as Secretary of Homeland Security shortly after the 2004 elections, but last week [in August 2009] he revealed that there was much more to the story.

Politics or Security?

In a forthcoming book, Ridge complains that the weekend before Election Day, [George W.] Bush administration officials leaned on him to raise the color-coded threat level. Dismayed, Ridge refused the demand, and concluded he needed to resign. "I wondered," Ridge writes, "Is this about security or politics?"

That's a question we ought to ask about DHS [the Department of Homeland Security] as a whole. Since its creation in 2003, the department has done little to provide genuine security and much to encourage a pernicious politics of fear. We'd be better off without it.

The Homeland Security Advisory System is a case in point. Even before Ridge's revelation, two separate studies showed that Bush received a boost to his approval ratings with each escalation of the terror threat level. The warning has been raised above yellow ("elevated") 16 times, but it's never been lowered to blue or green, the bottom rungs on DHS's Ladder of Fear. Yet, with Spinal Tap[1] logic ("this goes to 11!") the department insists on keeping all five levels.

The department itself is a dog's breakfast [i.e., a mishmash] of 22 federal agencies brought together in the hope of providing better coordination on a common mission. But turf

---

1. *This Is Spinal Tap* was a 1984 faux documentary about the band Spinal Tap. One skit involved an amplifier that had 11, rather than 10, volume settings.

battles left key antiterror agencies like the FBI out of the reorganization, and DHS finished last or next to last on every measure of employee morale in a 2006 Office of Personnel Management study.

Inefficiency and Waste

The truth, as analyst Jeffrey Rosen points out, is that DHS is 'an institutional money pit that has more to do with symbols than substance.' Indeed, a congressional investigation in 2008 documented some $15 billion in failed contracts that have run wildly over budget or been cancelled before completion.

Many of the contracts that DHS considers a success have funded a growing federal assault on privacy. The fishing village of Dillingham, AK (pop. 2,400), is too small for a streetlight, but thanks to a homeland security grant, it now has 80 surveillance cameras.

The town of Ridgely, MD (pop. 1,400), got a grant for cameras as well. "It was difficult to be able to find something to use the money for," said Ridgely's police chief, but "if you don't ask, you aren't going to get a thing."

Other homeland security grants have gone toward the development of the Transportation Security Administration's "nude scanner," which should add a whole new level of indignity to the airport security line experience, in which we're already poked and prodded, and warned not to joke about the poking.

True enough, even if DHS were abolished, it wouldn't make government much smaller. Most of the department's 200,000 employees work for agencies—Customs [and Border Protection], the Coast Guard, INS [Immigration and Naturalization Service, now Immigration and Customs Enforcement (ICE)]—that would survive DHS's closure. (Though we could at least stop work on the hideous, 38-acre, $4 billion Nebraska Avenue Complex currently, being built in Southeast [Washington,] DC).

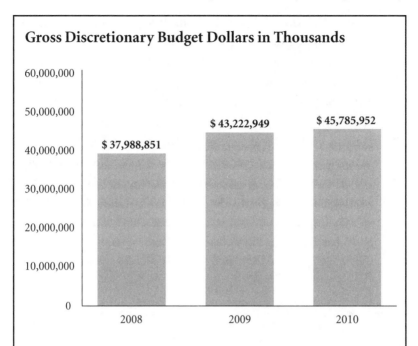

Gross Discretionary Budget Dollars in Thousands

TAKEN FROM: U.S. Department of Homeland Security, "Budget-in-Brief: Fiscal Year 2010," U.S. Department of Homeland Security Website, 2009, http://www.dhs.gov.

Important Bipartisan Symbolism

Shuttering DHS would be largely symbolic; but symbolism matters. Down to its very name—an "abhorrently un-American, odiously Teutono/Soviet term," in the words of [*Atlantic Monthly* writer] James Fallows—the Department of Homeland Security has stood for bureaucratic centralization in an atmosphere of permanent crisis.

In this season of angry town hall meetings liberals have taken to defending the [April 2009] overwrought DHS memo warning about "Rightwing Extremism." But for all his faults, "No Drama" [President Barack] Obama has resisted the temptation to boost his popularity by stoking domestic terror fears or goosing the threat level. But, as his popularity falls, that option may look increasingly attractive.

In July [2009], DHS secretary Janet Napolitano announced the formation of a bipartisan commission to review the terror alert system, perhaps seeking political cover to scrap it in its current form. That's good news. But one wishes Congress had the political will to scrap the department as a whole.

Once upon a time, some 15 years ago [in the mid-1990s], "reform" meant trying to get rid of useless, liberty-threatening cabinet departments. If the GOP [the Republican Party] ever recovers that spirit, they could do worse than starting with the DHS.

> "Since its inception, [the Department
> of Homeland Security] has had to deal
> with federal agencies and authorities
> necessary to carry out the homeland
> security mission being kept outside the
> department."

The Department of Homeland Security Should Be Given More Power

Josh Filler

Josh Filler is the former director of the Office of State and Local Government Coordination for the Department of Homeland Security (DHS). In the following viewpoint, he argues that DHS was intended to consolidate counterterrorism organizations. This goal was never achieved, he says, because the FBI was kept out of the agency. Without the FBI, Filler argues, DHS has little ability to investigate terrorist threats, which undermines its role in protecting against them. Filler concludes that DHS and antiterrorism activities in general would be more effective if the FBI were made part of DHS.

Josh Filler, "Homeland Protection Zone—the Disconnect Between DHS and the Homeland Security Mission," *Emergency Management*, February 15, 2010. Reproduced by permission.

As you read, consider the following questions:

1. According to Filler, what did the FBI fear might happen if it entered DHS?
2. The author says that the Secret Service is unique in what way?
3. With what other agencies in the Justice Department has the FBI had numerous battles, according to Filler?

Recently, Dr. James Carafano of the Heritage Foundation wrote a piece entitled "Lay off [Janet] Napolitano and the Homeland Security Department," which includes a rundown of which federal agencies dropped the ball in the Christmas Day [2009] flight 253 "panty bomber" case. In his analysis, Carafano concludes that "none of the responsibility for keeping the attempted killer [Umar Farouk Abdulmutallab] off the plane rests with the Department of Homeland Security [DHS]."[1] This is a remarkable statement primarily because it's true, which raises a serious question: How is it we have a Department of Homeland Security that is not actually responsible for much of our homeland security?

Not Enough Consolidation

When DHS was created it was marketed as a consolidation of key counter-terrorism agencies and functions that had previously been spread incoherently throughout the government. However, in the end, while several agencies and functions did come into DHS, as outlined in Carafano's article, all too many did not. This includes issuing visas (State Department), managing the No Fly List (FBI), and serving as the hub for homeland security intelligence (National Counter Terrorism Center). All of this has caused confusion from the start, which Congress and both the [George W.] Bush and [Barack] Obama

1. On December 25, 2009, Umar Farouk Abdulmutallab was arrested for attempting to blow up Northwest Airlines Flight 253 headed to Detroit with explosives concealed in his underwear.

Administrations have compounded by making the DHS Secretary the face of homeland security for appearances, but in function relegating DHS to junior partner in the conglomerate of federal counter-terrorism agencies.

Perhaps no case better exemplifies the disconnect between DHS and the larger homeland security mission than the decision to keep the FBI out of the new department. Even before the flight 253 attack, Fox News ran a story outlining the internal fighting between the FBI and DHS on matters involving information sharing with state and local law enforcement generally and the recent Naji Bullazazi case in particular.[2]

Chaos and Fear

In 2002, when the creation of DHS was being debated, the issue of whether the FBI should be inside the new department garnered much attention. Some would argue the FBI fought as hard against becoming a part of DHS as it has in fighting al-Qaeda [terrorist organization responsible for the September 11, 2001, attacks]. All kidding aside, why did the FBI resist going into DHS back in 2002? Two reasons perhaps best summarize the answer: chaos and fear of the unknown.

To understand the FBI's fears of going into DHS one need only look to the U.S. Customs Service, or rather the former U.S Customs Service. The Customs Service had been intact since 1789, but upon its entry into DHS the U.S. Customs Service as we knew it is gone, split into two parts with its investigators now working with former INS [Immigration and Naturalization Service] investigators at the new Immigration and Customs Enforcement and its inspectors working with the Border Patrol at the new Customs and Border Protection.

In addition to the FBI's fear of being disbanded, there was the inevitable chaos surrounding the establishment of DHS. In 2002, the Bureau was going through very painful

2. Bullazazi was arrested in 2009 as part of a group accused of planning suicide bombings in New York City.

reorganizations of its own and the weight of the two events, internal reorganization and external placement in a new department, may have proven too much for the FBI while it was being charged with preventing the next attack inside the homeland.

A Conflict of National Security Interest

Despite the FBI's fears, there is an inherent conflict in having the primary responsibility to prevent and protect against terrorism separate from the primary responsibility to investigate and counter terrorism. Indeed, the primary mission of the FBI is to "protect and defend the United States against terrorist and foreign intelligence threats." Under the Homeland Security Act of 2002, the primary mission of DHS is "to prevent terrorist attacks within the United States." However, the 2002 Act goes on to specify that "primary responsibility for investigating and prosecuting acts of terrorism shall be vested not in the Department, but rather in Federal, State, and local law enforcement agencies with jurisdiction over acts of terrorism." That clause, coupled with the FBI being kept out of DHS, has been a major factor in the division between DHS and the means to carry out its mission.

The U.S. Secret Service, a DHS component, actually presents a case study on the issue of separating investigations from security, as well as what the FBI's placement in DHS could have looked like. Under the Homeland Security Act, the Secret Service was placed into DHS with the caveat that it had to be "maintained as a distinct entity within the Department" meaning it could not be disbanded the way Customs was.

As a law enforcement agency, the Secret Service is unique in many ways, particularly in that the success of one its core missions, protecting the President, Vice President, etc. (protectees) is achieved if it prevents attacks against those protectees. The purpose of investigating all threats against the President is to prevent the threats from materializing into actual attacks. No investigation is judged a "success" if a President is assassinated and the assassin is subsequently arrested, prosecuted and convicted. Coincidentally, the FBI leads the investigation into such actual attacks.

In its 1964 report on the assassination of President [John F.] Kennedy, the Warren Commission, in evaluating the different federal agencies and their respective roles and responsibilities in protecting the President, noted that removing the responsibility for investigating threats against the President from the Secret Service and placing that function in a different federal agency, notably the FBI, could undermine the Secret Service's fundamental role of protection.

It is suggested that an organization shorn of its power to investigate all the possibilities of danger to the President and becoming merely the recipient of information gathered by others would become limited solely to acts of physical alertness and personal courage incident to its responsibilities. So circumscribed, it could not maintain the esprit de corps or the necessary alertness for this unique and challenging responsibility.

Concerning the flight 253 attack, Secretary Napolitano recently told Congress that DHS is largely a "consumer" of intelligence when it comes to homeland security. This is correct and precisely the situation the Warren Commission warned against concerning the Secret Service. The decision [to] keep the FBI out of DHS has effectively separated prevention from protection where the protectee is the United States itself.

The FBI Should Be Placed in DHS

Placing the FBI in DHS would not miraculously remove all of the conflicts over jurisdiction, roles and responsibilities between the Bureau and the current DHS operational components. The FBI has had numerous such battles over the years with sister Justice Department agencies including the DEA [Drug Enforcement Administration] and ATF [Bureau of Alcohol, Tobacco, Firearms, and Explosives]. Battles over jurisdiction and turf are an art form in Washington, particularly within the intelligence and law enforcement communities, regardless of where they sit on an organization chart.

Nonetheless, if we truly wanted a single agency whose primary mission was the protection of the homeland from terrorism, placing the FBI in DHS would have made that aspiration closer to a reality. It also would have more closely aligned federal law enforcement organization with state and local law enforcement organization, which more often separates the prosecutors from the police and investigators.

Organizational charts do matter. Clear lines of authority and responsibility are foundational elements for the success of any entity. Since its inception, DHS has had to deal with federal agencies and authorities necessary to carry out the homeland security mission being kept outside the department. The flight 253 case is just another reminder of this fact.

While DHS does play an important role in the current homeland security structure, it is a far cry from how it was marketed during its founding, as well as how it's perceived by the public today. This adversely impacts both public confidence in the department and actual operations.

Whether federal agencies or functions are ever consolidated in the department charged with leading the unified national effort to secure the homeland is anyone's guess. In the meantime, the disconnect between the homeland security mission and the department established to lead it will continue.

> *"All the institutions we have built since 9/11 are a lasting legacy that will give future generations and future Presidents the instruments they need to keep our country safe."*

Intelligence Gathering Has Improved Since 9/11

George W. Bush

George W. Bush is the forty-third president of the United States (2001–2009). In the following viewpoint, taken from an address to the employees of the Department of Homeland Security, he argues that the measures taken after the terrorist attacks of September 11, 2001, have helped to keep the United States safe. In particular, Bush says that the creation of the Department of Homeland Security has helped the country upgrade and coordinate security measures. This, he says, has resulted in improvements in a number of areas, including border security, emergency preparedness, and emergency management.

As you read, consider the following questions:

1. What does Bush say the United States has done to make its borders more secure?

George W. Bush, "President Bush Commemorates Fifth Anniversary of U.S. Department of Homeland Security," *U.S. Customs and Border Protection*, CBP.gov, March 6, 2008.

2. How does the author say that the federal government sent threat information to local authorities prior to 9/11, and how does he say things have changed since 9/11?

3. How does Bush say his administration transformed the Federal Bureau of Investigation?

B efore [the terrorist attacks of] 9/11 [2001], there was no single department of government charged with protecting the homeland. So we undertook the most sweeping reorganization of the federal government since the start of the Cold War. We merged 22 different government organizations into a single department with a clear mission: Secure America and protect the American people from future attacks.

DHS Protects America

The past five years [2003–2008], the men and women of [the Department of Homeland Security (DHS)] have carried out that mission with skill and determination. In ways seen and unseen, you work each day to protect our people from dangerous and determined enemies. I know how hard you work; a lot of Americans don't. And perhaps, on this fifth anniversary, the message will get through that there's a lot of dedicated, decent, honorable folks working their hearts out to protect the country.

The Department of Homeland Security is working to stop terrorists from infiltrating our country. On 9/11, America was attacked from within, by 19 men who entered our country, hid among us, and then killed thousands. To stop this from happening again we've taken important steps to prevent dangerous people from entering America. We made our borders more secure and deployed new technologies for screening people entering America.

We're on track to double the number of Border Patrol agents to serve our country. . . . We've unified our terrorism databases into one central database. We are enhancing it with biometric capabilities [the capability to recognize physical characteristics, such as fingerprints]. We've improved the way we evaluate visa applicants. We made it harder to counterfeit travel documents. We want to know who's coming to our country, and who's leaving our country, and we take significant steps to be able to tell the American people the answer to those questions.

Secondly, the Department of Homeland Security is working to stop terrorists from smuggling biological and chemical and nuclear weapons into our cities. The department has deployed a layered system of protections against these dangerous materials that starts overseas, continues along our borders, and extends throughout our country. We've launched innovative programs to protect major metropolitan areas by providing early detection of biological, or nuclear, or radiological attacks. We are determined to stop the world's most dangerous men from striking America with the world's most dangerous weapons.

The Department of Homeland Security is working to protect our transportation systems and other critical infrastructure from terrorist attacks. Our enemies have declared—they have made it abundantly clear that if they can strike economic targets here in America, they can terrorize our people and do great harm to our economy. So in the face of this threat, the Department of Homeland Security has taken decisive action. Since 9/11, we've worked with the private sector to develop comprehensive security plans for 17 of the nation's critical sectors—including our food and water supplies, chemical and nuclear facilities, power grids and telecommunications networks.

Under Operation Neptune Shield, the men and women of the Coast Guard are protecting more than 360 ports, and more than 95,000 miles of coastline. We've taken action to protect our transportation systems—including a massive over-

The Mission of DHS

[The Department of Homeland Security (DHS)] is by far the youngest department of the federal government, even though now it is the largest department of the federal government, comprising 210,000 employees across our country with a very, very broad mission to prevent our country from being attacked—either through terrorists or other man-caused disaster—but also to prepare our country and to be able to respond to whatever kind of disaster, man-caused or natural, with strength, efficiency, resilience, and to recover in the best way possible, to restore people and communities back to where they were before a catastrophe occurred. So we are there to protect and prevent.

Janet Napolitano, Department of Homeland Security website, March 16, 2009. www.dhs.gov.

haul of security at our airports, and new steps to protect our railways and mass transit systems.

The message should be clear to the American people: We will protect our country; we will protect our economy from those who seek to do us harm.

Strengthening Defenses

The Department of Homeland Security is working to strengthen our defenses against cyber attacks. Our enemies understand that America's economy relies on uninterrupted use of the Internet—and that a devastating attack in cyberspace would be a massive blow to our economy and way of life. And so we've taken steps to enhance our cyber security; created a new National Cyber Security Division in this department, charged with protecting against virtual terrorism. We've established a Computer Emergency Readiness Team to provide 24-hour watch—so we can stop cyber attacks before they spread and cripple our economy. The United States Secret Service has established 24 Electronic Crimes Task Forces with a mission to prevent, detect, and investigate cyber attacks on our country.

As we protect our cyber networks, we're also working to deny our enemies the use of the Internet to recruit and train operatives and plan attacks on America. Our strategy is to deny the terrorists safe haven anywhere in the world—and that includes a virtual safe haven on the Internet.

The Department of Homeland Security is working to strengthen cooperation with state and local governments—so we can prevent terrorist attacks, and respond effectively if we have to. Before 9/11, the federal government sent threat information to authorities—local authorities—by fax machine. Today, we've established 21st century lines of communication that allow us to share classified threat information rapidly and securely. We've helped state and local officials establish intelligence fusion centers in 46 states. These centers allow federal officials to provide intelligence to our state and local partners, and allow locally-generated information to get to officials here in Washington who need it.

Even all these steps—with even all these steps, we know that in a free society—there's no such thing as perfect security. That's the challenge. To attack us, the terrorists only have to be right once; to stop them, we need to be right 100 percent of the time. And so we're working to ensure that if attack does occur, this country is ready. We'll do everything we can to stop attacks—and we are. I can confidently tell the American people, a lot of folks are working hard to protect them, with a good, comprehensive strategy.

But if the enemy is able to make it here and attack us, we want to be able to respond. And so since September of 2001, we've provided more than $23 billion of equipment and training, and other critical needs for America's state and local first responders. We want people at the local level prepared.

Improving Emergency Response

We've worked with officials in 75 major metropolitan areas to improve the ability of first responders to communicate clearly in an emergency. We've helped establish mutual aid agreements within states, and strengthened the Emergency Management [Assistance] Compact among states—so that when communities need help from their neighbors, the right assistance will get to the right people at the right time.

We've greatly expanded the nation's stockpile of drugs and vaccines that would be needed in the event of a bioterrorist attack or a mass casualty incident. We now have enough smallpox vaccine for every American in case of an emergency. We've increased our investments in bio-defense medical research and development at the National Institutes of Health by more than 3,000 percent since 2001. We launched Project BioShield—an effort to speed the development of new vaccines and treatments against biological agents that could be used in a terrorist attack.

We've learned from our mistakes to improve our response when disaster strikes. When Hurricane Katrina hit our nation's Gulf Coast [in 2005], it exposed weaknesses in America's emergency response capabilities. So we retooled and restructured FEMA [Federal Emergency Management Agency]. Since Hurricane Katrina, we've improved FEMA's logistics management, strengthened its operations planning, augmented disaster assistance programs, and provided the agency with additional personnel and resources.

And we have seen outstanding results as a result of these efforts. FEMA's response to the [2007] California wildfires, to the [2007] Minneapolis bridge collapse, and the tornadoes that struck the Mississippi Valley [in February 2008] were exemplary. . . . Because of these efforts, FEMA and Homeland

Security are better prepared. There's still work to do, but we're doing it. We're never satisfied here in the Department of Homeland Security. We're constantly assessing weaknesses and needs, and constantly adjusting, because there's no greater calling than to protect our country.

Building Institutions

The Department of Homeland Security is vital to our safety, and it's just one of the institutions that have been built or transformed to keep our nation safe: We created the new Office of Director of National Intelligence, which led a broad restructuring of our nation's intelligence agencies for the threats of the 21st century. We transformed the FBI into an agency whose primary focus is stopping terrorism, and reorganized the Department of Justice to help combat the threat.

We created the National Counterterrorism Center—where members of this department, as well as the FBI and the CIA [Central Intelligence Agency] and other departments and agencies, work side by side to track terrorist threats and prevent new attacks.

We created the Proliferation Security Initiative—a coalition of more than 85 nations that are working together to stop shipments of weapons of mass destruction, their delivery systems, and related materials.

And to find out what the terrorists know about planned attacks, we established a program run by the CIA to detain and question key terrorist leaders and operatives. . . .

The men and women of the Department of Homeland Security can be proud of all that you have accomplished in five years. I've just laid out some of that which you've accomplished, and it took me about 30 minutes. You have built a vital and effective department that is helping to prevent dangerous enemies from striking our people. Your efforts, and all the institutions we have built since 9/11, are a lasting legacy that will give future generations and future Presidents the instruments they need to keep our country safe.

The most important legacy we can leave behind is a commitment to remain vigilant. With the passage of time, the memories of September the 11th have grown more distant. For some, there is temptation to think that the threats to our country have grown distant, as well. They haven't. And our job is to never forget the threat—and to implement strategies that will protect the homeland from those who seek [to do] us harm.

"We were led to believe the intelligence situation had improved in the wake of 9/11, but . . . we have no evidence of significant change."

Intelligence Gathering Has Not Improved Since 9/11

Melvin A. Goodman

Melvin A. Goodman is a senior fellow at the Center for International Policy and an adjunct professor of government at the Johns Hopkins University. In the following viewpoint, he argues that the December 25, 2009, terrorist bombing attempt demonstrates that the U.S. intelligence community is incompetent. He blames bureaucratic confusion, poor intelligence sharing, and poor leadership for both the Christmas bombing incident and the 9/11 attacks and argues that the 9/11 Commission's recommendations actually worsened the problems in the intelligence community. He concludes that major reforms are needed, though unlikely to occur.

As you read, consider the following questions:

1. What warnings about potential terrorist bombing plots does Goodman say the United States received prior to 9/11?

Melvin A. Goodman, "9/11 and Christmas 2009: Two Examples of a Failure of Intelligence," *Truthout*, January 4, 2010. Reproduced by permission.

2. The author says the Department of Homeland Security should have been abolished following what event?

3. According to Goodman, which U.S. agencies or departments keep lists of terrorism suspects?

O ne week after the attacks on the World Trade Center and the Pentagon [on September 11, 2001], National Security Adviser Condoleezza Rice told the press corps, "This isn't Pearl Harbor." No, it was worse.

Movement Without Improvement

In 1941, the United States didn't have a director of central intelligence, 14 intelligence agencies and an overall intelligence budget of more than $50 billion to provide early warning of enemy attack. One day after a Nigerian man nearly blew an airliner out of the sky,[1] Director of Homeland Security Janet Napolitano and White House spokesman Robert Gibbs told the media that the system had worked. No, the system was dysfunctional.

In 2009, we had two additional intelligence agencies, a czar for national intelligence and an intelligence budget of more than $75 billion. In all three cases, there was sufficient intelligence available to prevent the attacks. In all three cases, however, our intelligence efforts were unimaginative, divided and diffuse.

A blizzard of warnings went unheeded in all three cases. The United States had broken the Japanese military code, which provided many warnings of a decision to attack the United States. In the case of 9/11 [2001], the Central Intelligence Agency [CIA] received warnings from foreign liaison intelligence services, including the French, German, Israeli and Russian services.

The German intelligence service warned both the CIA and Mossad, the Israeli service, in the summer of 2001 that

1. On December 25, 2009, Umar Farouk Abdulmutallab was arrested for attempting to blow up a Northwest Airlines flight with explosives concealed in his underwear.

terrorists were planning to hijack commercial aircraft and use them as weapons to attack US targets. The Israelis issued their own warnings to the FBI and the CIA in August 2001 that [terrorist organization] al-Qaeda was planning to attack US targets. The State Department and the CIA even possessed information that al-Qaeda had decided on targeting American Airlines and United Airlines, prompting some Foreign Service officers to change travel plans.

Warnings Remain Unheeded

As early as August 2009, the CIA and the National Security Agency [NSA] had sensitive information on a person of interest dubbed the "Nigerian," [the underwear bomber] who was suspected of meeting with terrorist elements in Yemen. The mainstream media are treating Yemen as a new concern, but Yemen has been a problem for terrorism for the past ten years.

[Admiral] Tony Zinni had been warned in 2000 not to refuel ships off the Yemeni coast, but chose to ignore these warnings. The USS *Cole* was attacked in October 2000. A prominent Nigerian banker and former senior government official, well known to the international community, relayed suspicions about his son to the US Embassy and the CIA station in Lagos, [Nigeria,] but there was no effort to approach Yemeni officials to gather information on the banker's son, Umar Farouk Abdulmutallab.

The son was a poster child for the "no fly" list, buying his ticket with cash, checking no luggage, lying to British authorities about his student visa and spending several months in Yemen. The British denied Abdulmutallab reentry, but the US State Department didn't even bother to check whether he had an entry visa for the United States.

In fact, he had a multiple entry visa and, since all intelligence and law enforcement agencies have access to State's consular database listing visa holders, this fact was available throughout the community. It's one thing to worry about due process in dealing with a US citizen; it makes no sense to wait for additional derogatory information in the case of a foreigner who has traveled to Yemen and whose father has provided a warning about his son's extremism.

Failure to Share Intelligence

The simple fact is that the intelligence community is not a "community"; it does not share intelligence effectively and it fails to make corporate decisions. The NSA had transcripts of al-Qaeda phone conversations in 2001 and sensitive intercepts on the "Nigerian" in 2009 that it didn't share with the CIA, the FBI or the National Security Council [NSC]. The FBI accumulated intelligence on al-Qaeda that it hoped to use in a criminal case against [al-Qaeda leader] Osama bin Laden; therefore, most of this intelligence never left the compartmented areas of FBI headquarters. The CIA withheld information on two 9/11 terrorists, presumably because it hoped to recruit these suspects as sources.

We were led to believe the intelligence situation had improved in the wake of 9/11, but in view of the traditional cultural and professional jealousies of the military and civilian intelligence agencies, we have no evidence of significant change. Various departments and agencies have their own watch lists for limiting travel of terrorist suspects, but apply their own parochial concerns to operational activities and often ignore the intelligence products of rival agencies.

The master list at the National Counter Terrorist Center is too large and unwieldy (more than 550,000 names) to be useful, and the State Department computer network lacks an automatic feedback loop that would link a suspect to a US visa. The Department of Homeland Security [DHS] never should have been created and should have been abolished in the wake of Hurricane Katrina (remember "you're doing a heck of a job, Brownie").[2] If we must have such a superfluous organization, then it should possess a centralized depository of terrorist suspects containing all relevant information.

The analytical capabilities of the CIA, the FBI and the DHS have not been enhanced by the creation of the intelligence czar. Moreover, it is revealing that President Barack Obama made his decision last month [in December 2009] to increase troops in Afghanistan without requesting a National Intelligence Estimate from the so-called intelligence community. Perhaps, he understands that there are too many instances where assumptions drive facts in the intelligence process.

The Fault of the 9/11 Commission

Former members of the 9/11 Commission are claiming that their recommendations have not been fully implemented, but it was the 9/11 Commission that helped to create the crazy-quilt intelligence organization that we now have, with too many working parts and a cumbersome bureaucracy. The Commission is responsible for the creation of the Director of National Intelligence (DNI), a sclerotic and bloated bureaucracy that has done little to improve strategic intelligence, and the National Counter Terrorism Center (NCTC), which is at the center of the Nigerian intelligence failure. Hurricane Katrina in 2005 demonstrated DHS is dysfunctional; the Nigerian failure teaches us that the DNI and the NCTC need reform.

The 9/11 Commission's creation of an intelligence czar has ensured that diversity and competition in collection and analysis of intelligence will be given short shrift. Truth is elusive within the intelligence process, and there is rarely a single answer to a controversial question or problem. The best

2. Hurricane Katrina was a 2005 storm that decimated New Orleans. The DHS's response to the crisis was widely perceived as inadequate, despite President George W. Bush's praise of Michael Dewayne Brown ("Brownie"), a DHS official in charge of emergency management.

intelligence analysis often comes from contrarian thinkers, but the militarized intelligence process rewards consensus and not competition.

In the one area where we need centralization, watch lists for terrorist suspects, we have a redundancy of collections. Homeland Security keeps one list for border crossings; the State Department has a list for visas; the Transportation Security Administration has a no-fly list and a selectee list with 4,000 and 14,000 listings, respectively; and the National Counter Terrorism Center has an unwieldy database of 550,000 names. The criteria for each list differ, and it takes an interagency group to determine whether to place an individual on a specific list.

Our Luck Will Not Last

There is at least one thing we have to be thankful for. In view of the failed efforts of Richard Reid [who failed in an attempt to light an explosive concealed in his shoe while on board an aircraft] in 2001 and Abdulmutallab, we can be thankful al-Qaeda still has not perfected an effective detonator. We should also applaud the post-9/11 reforms that limited the amounts of liquid that can be taken on commercial aircraft.

The United States may not be so lucky the next time around, so President Obama must take a hard look at his entire national security team, particularly CIA Director Leon Panetta, DNI Dennis Blair, and NSC Deputy Director John Brennan, to make sure they are taking the necessary actions to reform the process. The failure points seem obvious, with bad decisions being made at a relatively low level in the process. The president has not demonstrated an interest in reforming the intelligence community, however, despite his campaign rhetoric.

Ironically, the president has left the CIA without its most effective component for investigating failure because he hasn't named a statutory inspector general for the CIA to replace

John Helgerson, who announced his retirement ten months ago [in March 2009]. Helgerson was responsible for the most authoritative investigation of the 9/11 failure, which the [George W.] Bush administration and the CIA managed to cover up.

Periodical Bibliography

The following articles have been selected to supplement the diverse views presented in this chapter.

Jill R. Aitoro
"DHS Needs Power to Compel Agencies to Fix Security Holes," Nextgov, June 16, 2010. www.nextgov.com/nextgov/ ng_20100616_1933.php?.

Dennis C. Blair
"Strengthening Our Nation's Front Line of Defense," *Washington Post*, December 18, 2009. www.washingtonpost.com/wp-dyn/content/ article/2009/12/17/AR2009121703672.html.

Tom Burghardt
"New Director of National Intelligence: Overseeing Aggression Abroad and Repression at Home," GlobalResearch.ca, June 7, 2010.

Elbridge A. Colby
"Making Intelligence Smart," *Policy Review*, August 1, 2007. www.hoover.org/publications/ policy-review/article/5843.

Department of Homeland Security
"Department of Homeland Security: Progess in Implementing 9/11 Commission Recommendations," July 22, 2009. www.dhs.gov/xlibrary/ assets/9-11-commission-update-report-7-22- 10.pdf.

Melvin A. Goodman
"One More Feckless Study on Intelligence Reform," *Public Record*, September 17, 2009.

Ronald Kessler
"Abolish the Office of the Director of National Intelligence," Newsmax.com, May 21, 2010. www.newsmax.com/RonaldKessler/dni-leon- panetta-director/2010/05/21/id/359749.

Terry Kivlan
"Former Senator Decries DHS a 'Mess,' Urges Reorganization," *Government Executive*, December 4, 2007.

Jeffrey Rosen
"Man-Made Disaster," *New Republic*, December 24, 2008.

Veronique du Rugy
"Are We Ready for the Next 9/11?" *Reason*, March 2006.

Noah Shachtman   "DHS Geek Squad: No Power, No Plan, Lots of Vacancies," Danger Room blog, June 16, 2010. www.wired.com/dangerroom/2010/06/dhs-geek-squad-understaffed-with-no-juice-and-no-plan/.

Does the U.S. Intelligence Community Advance Domestic Security?

Chapter Preface

On May 1, 2010, "a crude car bomb . . . was discovered in a smoking Nissan Pathfinder in the heart of [New York's] Time Square . . . prompting the evacuation of thousands of tourists and theatergoers," according to Al Baker and William K. Rashbaum writing in that day's *New York Times*. The bomb did not explode, and no one was injured. A few days later, a U.S. citizen of Pakistani descent named Faisal Shahzad was arrested in connection with the bombing attempt when officials pulled him off a flight to Dubai. In June, Shahzad pleaded guilty to planting the bomb. He also said that he had received "five days of training with the Pakistan Taliban" and that the Taliban gave him money to fund his bombing effort, according to a 2010 article by Shira Bush on the Liveshots blog.

Some commentators have argued that the capture and confession of Shahzad indicated the successful operation of law enforcement and U.S. intelligence. Daphne Eviatar writing in a 2010 article on the Human Rights First blog, noted that "what's critical about this case is that skilled law enforcement officials knew that even though his attempt failed, Shahzad was a potential treasure trove of information about the Pakistani Taliban and their operations. And they've exploited that well: after his arrest, Shahzad reportedly cooperated with law enforcement and answered their questions for two weeks before even requesting a lawyer. His arraignment was postponed several times even after a lawyer was appointed to represent him, indicating that even with a lawyer he continued to cooperate." Shahzad's cooperation led to the arrest of a Pakistani army major who may have been involved in the plot. It also led to several additional arrests in the United States.

Other commentators have argued that the Times Square bombing attempt revealed intelligence weaknesses. Senator John McCain, a leading Republican, argued that authorities should not have read Shahzad his Miranda rights after arresting him. Another complaint was expressed by Scott Carmichael writing in a 2010 article on Gadling.com. Carmichael argued that Shahzad's arrest demonstrated a failure of airline security, since Shahzad was able to actually board a plane before the FBI arrested him. As Carmichael noted, Shahzad "had been added to the no-fly list, but the airline failed to check the most recent version of the list." Kim R. Holmes, in a 2010 article on the Heritage Foundation's website, added that while "law enforcement officers did a good job after the fact, apprehending Mr. Shahzad before he got away," they could have and should have done better in preventing the bomb from being planted in the first place.

The following viewpoints will consider and evaluate the effectiveness of domestic security measures in preventing incidents such as the Times Square bombing attempt and in apprehending and obtaining information from terrorists.

> "[Before warrantless wiretaps were allowed] as much as two thirds of potential intelligence from U.S. eavesdropping capabilities was being lost."

Warrantless Wiretaps Are Needed to Protect Against Terrorism

Mortimer B. Zuckerman

Mortimer B. Zuckerman is the editor in chief of U.S. News & World Report *and the publisher of the* New York Daily News. *In the following viewpoint, he argues that terrorists pose an extremely dangerous threat to national security, and that free societies like the United States are especially vulnerable to them. He says that current restrictions on wiretapping make it difficult for the United States to collect important intelligence. He concludes that the warrantless wiretapping bill proposed by the George W. Bush administration includes reasonable safeguards for privacy while making it easier to trace and stop terrorists.*

As you read, consider the following questions:

1. According to Zuckerman, how were terrorists in London planning to avoid airport security?

Mortimer B. Zuckerman, "The Case for Surveillance," *U.S. News & World Report,* August 26, 2007. Reproduced by permission.

2. What is FISA, and what restrictions did it place on U.S. intelligence capability, according to the author?

3. Why does Zuckerman say that some telecommunications companies have stopped cooperating with the National Security Agency?

How does any civilized nation cope with fanatical barbarism? What kind of people will plot to murder thousands—so crazed with hate they will kill their own families for the cause? Even after 9/11 we have been slow to recognize the nature of the beast we face. It is hard for us to comprehend the mentality of, say, the group of 21 homegrown suicidal jihadists apprehended [in 2006] in Britain. We now know not only that they were prepared to blow up 10 civilian airliners flying from London to the United States—which might have killed as many as 3,500 innocent people—but also that they planned to avoid airport scrutiny by traveling with their wives and children and were thus prepared to execute their nearest and dearest.

Freedom Makes Us Vulnerable

As a free society, we are remarkably vulnerable. Our open borders permit second-generation terrorists from Europe to infiltrate under the legal visa waiver program. We admit many imams [Muslim clerics] from Egypt and Pakistan trained in Saudi Arabia under the extremist perversion of Islam known as Wahhabism. The consequences of our tolerance are spelled out in a [2007] report by the New York City Police Counterterrorism Department. It focuses on how difficult it is to follow the "trajectory of radicalization"—the behavior and whereabouts of homegrown radical Islamists. That New York report has to be read with the most recent National Intelligence Estimate that the external threat from al Qaeda [the terrorist organization responsible for the September 11, 2001, attacks] has not waned despite expanded worldwide counterterrorism efforts.

Warrantless Wiretapping Is Legal

A secret federal appeals court has said telecommunications companies must cooperate with the government to intercept international phone calls and e-mail of American citizens suspected of being spies or terrorists.

The ruling came in a case involving ... the president's ... power to conduct wiretapping without warrants for intelligence purposes.

James Risen and Eric Lichtban,
New York Times, *January 15, 2009.*

This is the context in which to consider the protests about tightening electronic surveillance, led by the liberal *New York Times* and the ultraliberal *New Yorker* and espoused by Democrats who watered down the recent reform legislation—including an insistence that it be reviewed in six months. How far should security concerns impinge on privacy? The administration [of President George W. Bush] says the balance has to be recalibrated. The trouble is that the administration has lost much of its moral authority. As *USA Today* put it, the White House "has all the credibility of a teenager who has squandered his allowance and is demanding more money."

True—but on this issue, it has a real case.

Until the law was changed, [al Qaeda leader Osama] bin Laden himself could have made a telephone call from Waziristan [in Pakistan] to Singapore and, if it were carried on a fiber optic cable that passes through the United States (as are the vast majority of long-distance calls), we would not have been able to listen without prior permission from the Foreign Intelligence Surveillance Act [FISA] court. FISA had to approve all interceptions of foreign-to-foreign communications coming through American wires, fiber optic cables, and switching stations. With warrants to the FISA court backed up, as much as two thirds of potential intelligence from U.S. eavesdropping capabilities was being lost. The director of national intelligence, Admiral Mike McConnell, gave Congress specific examples, such as one involving the capture of three American soldiers in Iraq.

Broader Powers Are Needed

Congress was right to eliminate the restrictions. Warrantless wiretaps will no longer be limited to "known foreign terrorists" but will include surveillance of the larger universe of "foreign targets," including America's enemies who are state actors and others not linked directly to al Qaeda, on the theory that if you can't find the needle, you have to examine the haystack.

Many of the Democrats supported the warrantless listening because they feared the political consequences of a terrorist attack occurring while they were on summer vacation—and because they had not taken the lead to plug the electronic intelligence gap. The Democrats have been politically vulnerable on national security and counterterrorism going back to the days of [President] Jimmy Carter, who was so naive about the intentions of the Soviet Union when it invaded Afghanistan [in 1979]. (And Carter is still willing to accommodate some of the most hostile enemies of the United States.)

Even now, Democrats are focusing on the scariest possible interpretation of the new law, ignoring its well-crafted rules to protect Americans. In addition to putting in the six-month expiration, they have failed to provide liability protection to U.S. telecommunication companies. Some of these have stopped cooperating with the National Security Agency since the program was exposed.

The Democrats should think again. Their concerns for American liberty are commendable, but if there is a serious terrorist attack, the outcry from the American public will force any government to enforce security measures that transform our way of life. We must have a bipartisan policy. The president would do well to work with leaders of Congress to agree jointly on an independent body to monitor the procedures. We have distinguished retired leaders who could do this. To allow essential security to become just a point of contention will only damage the country and the American people.

> *"[The Foreign Intelligence Security Act] actually allows secret, warrantless spying for up to 72 hours, which is more than sufficient for emergencies."*

Warrantless Wiretaps Are Not Needed to Protect Against Terrorism

The Left Coaster Blog

The Left Coaster is an established liberal group blog focusing on politics. In the following viewpoint, the author argues that the use of secret, warrantless wiretapping by the George W. Bush administration was unnecessary. The blog states that no terrorists were captured or thwarted by the warrantless wiretapping and that legal problems with warrantless wiretapping would make it difficult to prosecute any terrorists who were captured. The author also argues that existing wiretapping laws allowed for fast, flexible targeting of terrorist communications, and did not need to be circumvented.

As you read, consider the following questions:

1. According to The Left Coaster Blog, why is it wrong to say that the Foreign Intelligence Surveillance Act (FISA) unacceptably regulated wiretapping of calls from al Qaeda members overseas to Americans in the United States?

2. Why does the author argue that the 9/11 perpetrators would not have been considered "protected U.S. persons"?

3. Under what circumstances does The Left Coaster Blog say that FISA allows warrantless wiretapping?

[D]efenders of warrantless wiretapping say] Secret warrantless spying of Americans was/is required for national security reasons, since FISA [the Foreign Intelligence Surveillance Act] was inadequate and a bad law, and secret spying could have prevented 9/11.

TALKING POINT: Secret, *illegal, warrantless* spying on Americans enhances our national security.

FACT: Certainly *no more* than secret, *legal, warrant-based* spying; further, the illegal spying actually threatens America's national security because of the aid and comfort it gives to real terrorist supporters when they go to court (not [President George W.] Bush's Kangaroo courts[1] but the real court system in the United States). It also makes it easier to challenge Government prosecutions against *alleged* criminals.

TALKING POINT: The warrantless illegal spying was *required* because FISA unacceptably regulates wiretapping of calls from Al Qaeda [the terrorist group responsible for the September 11, 2001, attacks] members overseas to Americans in the U.S.

FACT: False. This is another bogus argument because *FISA does not apply to such calls at all.* As 14 constitutional scholars

---

1. George W. Bush established military courts to try some terrorists outside of the regular court system.

pointed out: "*FISA does not regulate electronic surveillance acquired abroad and targeted at non-U.S. persons, even if the surveillance happens to collect information on a communication with a U.S. person. Thus, the hypothetical tap on the Al Qaeda member abroad is not governed by FISA at all. FISA's requirements are triggered only when the surveillance is 'targeting [a] United States person who is in the United States,' or the surveillance 'acquisition occurs in the United States.'*"

TALKING POINT: The warrantless illegal spying was *required* because they had to monitor calls between Al Qaeda-affiliated individuals and Americans on U.S. soil.

FACT: False . . . As Glenn Greenwald notes: ". . . that defense makes no sense because eavesdropping on conversations involving al Qaeda members is *exactly* the circumstance in which it would be *most unnecessary* to bypass the FISA court. For that reason, the Administration's claim that it only eavesdropped on conversations involving al Qaeda members simply cannot be reconciled with the Administration's claimed need to operate outside of FISA, since if FISA allows anything, it would allow eavsdropping on al Qaeda."

Illegal Spying Has Not Prevented Terrorism

TALKING POINT: The illegal spying program was instrumental in revealing Al Qaeda plots within the U.S. and capturing Al Qaeda members.

FACT: False. As this [*New York Times*] report points out: "*The law enforcement and counterterrorism officials said the program had uncovered no active [al] Qaeda networks inside the United States planning attacks. There were no imminent plots—not inside the United States, the former F.B.I. official said.*" As the *New York Daily News* reported: "*The National Security Agency's [N.S.A.'s] secret domestic spying hasn't nabbed any Al Qaeda agents in the U.S. since the Sept. 11 attacks, FBI Director Robert Mueller told Congress yesterday.*" . . .

TALKING POINT: The illegal spying program could have roped in Zacarias Moussaoui or Mohammad Atta [two men involved in the 9/11 attacks] and prevented 9/11.

FACT: False . . . Moussaoui (and Atta) were foreign nationals to whom FISA already applied and a FISA warrant was not obtained in Moussaoui's case *because the Justice Department was not asked by the FBI to obtain a FISA warrant.* Moreover, as Frank Rich said . . . "*. . . [Vice President Dick Cheney] defended warrant-free wiretapping by saying it could have prevented the 9/11 attacks. Really? Not with this administration in charge. On 9/10 the N.S.A. (lawfully) intercepted messages in Arabic saying, "The match is about to begin," and, "Tomorrow is zero hour." You know the rest. Like all the chatter our government picked up during the president's excellent brush-clearing Crawford vacation of 2001 [Bush vacationed in Crawford, Texas, throughout August 2001], it was relegated to mañana; the N.S.A. didn't rouse itself to translate those warnings until 9/12.*" As William Arkin noted: "*The vice president fails to mention that the NSA actually did intercept communications indicating an event on 9/11, but didn't process it before that day. The FBI had reports about the hijackers, but it never put two and two together. The government had plenty of tip-offs and signals but it just wasn't focused enough or competent enough to competently carry out its constitutional duties.*" Further, as Think Progress notes, Bush himself claimed in June 2002 that 9/11 was not preventable!

TALKING POINT: Requiring FISA warrants may tip off our enemies.

FACT: This is again, unmitigated garbage, . . . (the FISA process is *always secret*).

Legal Arguments Inaccurate

TALKING POINT: FISA's "probable cause" standard for warrants was too restrictive and therefore did not allow the Jus-

The Importance of FISA

FISA and the FISA court and the process is so important because the intention of Congress in enacting the FISA statute was to do two things simultaneously: It was to protect the security of Americans, to keep them safe from the threats posed by hostile foreign powers and their agents; and it was also intended to protect the privacy of Americans, to protect them from intrusions into their privacy as well as to protect them from abuses of national security authorities that had taken place prior to the enactment of FISA. Congress was quite plain that that was the purpose of enacting the statute.

So what we do every day, really to my mind—and I've said this to our folks—is we're enacting and we're implementing this very important statute to achieve those two goals at the same time. That can be a very difficult job on a day-to-day basis. It's a lot of pressure. It's a very detailed statute, very intricate and yet extremely flexible. People, I think, don't really appreciate how flexible it is. At the same time it does impose a process that we have to comply with, and we enforce the laws enacted by Congress.

James Baker, Frontline, March 2, 2007. www.pbs.org.

tice Department (DoJ) to do the spying that was necessary.

FACT: False—the Bush administration/DoJ told Congress exactly the opposite in 2002.

TALKING POINT: FISA's 72-hour emergency window for wiretapping without a warrant was too cumbersome to use in practice and therefore not effective.

FACT: False—the Bush administration/DoJ told Congress exactly the opposite in 2002.

TALKING POINT: Many of the 9/11 perpetrators would have been considered "protected U.S. persons" per FISA.

FACT: False. Many of the hijackers were neither citizens nor permanent residents, and worse, were here illegally on *expired visas.*

TALKING POINT: There was insufficient evidence to get a FISA warrant in the case of Moussaoui. A federal judge barred the FBI from accessing Zacarias Moussaoui's computer.

FACT: False. . . .

TALKING POINT: The FISA law was inadequate and led to the FBI's not inspecting Moussaoui's personal effects.

FACT: False.

TALKING POINT: FISA's "probable cause" standard prevented the government from getting warrants in the Zacarias Moussaoui and Wen Ho Lee cases.

FACT: False. It was the FBI's (and DoJ's) misunderstanding of the FISA standard that prevented them from even asking for a warrant.

FISA Reform Was Not Needed

TALKING POINT: FISA required reform which had not happened even after 9/11.

FACT: False. Even though experts felt FISA required reform after 9/11, that already occurred via the Orwellian "PATRIOT" Act.[2] Further, as Glenn Greenwald has shown, the Bush administration themselves rejected a proposal in 2002 to amend the FISA law to make it much easier to spy on targets, saying that FISA was sufficient for what they were doing. . . .

TALKING POINT: The FISA statute is bad because it does not allow for immediate eavesdropping in emergencies. FISA requires getting a warrant before eavesdropping even for

---

2. The U.S.A. PATRIOT (Uniting and Strengthening America by Providing the Appropriate Tools Required to Intercept and Obstruct Terrorism) Act, enacted in October 2001, gave broad and unprecedented powers to law enforcement agencies.

emergencies and the administration did not have one or two days to put together the paperwork to get such a warrant or wait for a judge.

FACT: False . . . The truth is the opposite. FISA allows warrantless surveillance for up to 72 hours. Moreover, Bush has used emergency FISA wiretaps more often than all previous Presidents combined!

TALKING POINT: The FISA court is too bureaucratic and cannot be used in emergencies.

FACT: False, . . . FISA allows warrantless surveillance on U.S. persons for up to 72 hours and purely foreign agents for up to 1 year. Moreover, Bush has used emergency FISA wiretaps more often than all previous Presidents combined!

Further, as the *Washington Post* reported: "*Several FISA judges said they also remain puzzled by Bush's assertion that the court was not "agile" or "nimble" enough to help catch terrorists. . . . The court's actions in the days after the Sept. 11 attacks suggested that its judges were hardly unsympathetic to the needs of their nation at war. . . . On Sept. 12 . . . the requirement for detailed paperwork was greatly eased, allowing the NSA to begin eavesdropping the next day on anyone suspected of a link to al Qaeda, every person who had ever been a member or supporter of militant Islamic groups, and everyone ever linked to a terrorist watch list in the United States or abroad . . .*"

TALKING POINT: The FISA process is not fast or agile enough to catch terrorists or prevent terrorism.

FACT: False . . . In fact, FISA actually allows secret, warrantless spying for up to 72 hours, which is more than sufficient for emergencies and the FISA court has almost never rejected a request for a warrant. If the Bush administration wanted an extension to that they could have asked Congress to pass a FISA amendment. (Not to mention, it appears that the warrantless spying was started even without a Presidential Executive Order and possibly even before 9/11. If it was indeed started before 9/11, it certainly didn't prevent 9/11.)

TALKING POINT: "FISA requires the Attorney General to determine IN ADVANCE that a FISA application for that particular intercept will be fully supported and will be approved by the court before an emergency authorization may be granted. That review process can take precious time."

FACT: Another specious argument. The spying can begin *without this wait*, as long as the results of the spying are discarded if a warrant could not be obtained for it in the future. This is more than adequate for emergencies. . . .

TALKING POINT: "This is a different era, different war. It's a war where people are changing phone numbers and phone calls, and they're moving quick. And we've got to be able to detect and prevent" [a quote from President George W. Bush].

FACT: Highly misleading considering that FISA actually allows emergency wiretapping. Also . . . former CIA [Central Intelligence Agency] officer Larry Johnson . . . explains how U.S. intelligence agencies have in the past very successfully caught terrorists who keep switching phones, using roving wiretaps without having to break the law.

TALKING POINT: Terrorism is such a fundamentally new and unprecedented threat that it calls for extreme measures including giving up civil liberties.

FACT: False . . . (Other than revealing the fact that those making this argument are more often than not cowardly "bedwetters") the fact remains that the threat of terrorism, while substantial and requiring serious efforts to thwart it (as opposed to Bush's unprecedented incompetence on the matter), does not compare to the constant threat of large scale decimation during the Cold War. As former CIA officer Larry Johnson notes: *"The 'neo-conservative imperialists' live in a fantasy world where terrorism is the most deadly, horrific threat we* [have ever faced."]

> "The ... FBI's demand that Congress approve a huge expansion of their authority to obtain the sensitive Internet records of American citizens without a judge's approval is a brazen attack on civil liberties."

The FBI Is Abusing Its National Security Powers

Julian Sanchez

Julian Sanchez is a research fellow at the Cato Institute and a writer based in Washington, D.C. In the following viewpoint, he discusses the power that the FBI holds with its national security letters (NSLs). Sanchez notes that the scope of NSLs in regard to online activity is very unclear. In Sanchez's opinion, the demand of the FBI that Congress expand its authority to obtain citizens' Internet records—without the approval of a judge—threatens civil liberties. Seeking such power proves that the FBI and the current administration cannot and should not be trusted with it, Sanchez concludes.

Julian Sanchez, "Obama's Power Grab: The Obama Administration Wants to 'Clarify' FBI Power to Get Online Records Without Warrants—and Vastly Expand It," *The American Prospect*, July 29, 2010.

As you read, consider the following questions:

1. According to the author, what did national security letters (NSLs) originally allow investigators to obtain?

2. As argued by the Electronic Frontier Foundation, as cited by Sanchez, which constitutional amendment would be affected by broader authority of the FBI over the Internet?

3. According to the author, what did the Video Privacy Protection Act of 1988 do?

They're calling it a tweak—a "technical clarification"—but make no mistake: The Obama administration and the FBI's demand that Congress approve a huge expansion of their authority to obtain the sensitive Internet records of American citizens without a judge's approval is a brazen attack on civil liberties.

At issue is the scope of the Federal Bureau of Investigation'ss power to obtain information from "electronic communications service providers" using national security letters (NLS), which compel private companies to allow government access to communication records without a court order. The administration wants to add four words—"electronic communication transactional records"—to Section 2709 of the Electronic Communications Privacy Act, which spells out the types of communications data that can be obtained with an NSL. Yet those four little words would make a huge difference, potentially allowing investigators to draw detailed road maps of the online activity of citizens not even suspected of any connection to terrorism.

In their original form, NSLs were extremely narrow tools designed to allow federal investigators to obtain very basic telephone records (name, address, length of service, calls placed and received) that could be linked by "specific and articulable facts" to persons suspected of being terrorists or foreign spies. In 1993, Congress amended the statute to clarify that NSLs could be issued to electronic information service providers as well as traditional phone companies. But wary of the potential for misuse of what the House Judiciary Committee called this "extraordinary device" in a world of rapidly changing technology, Congress placed tight limits on the types of records that could be obtained, making clear that "new applications" of NSLs would be "disfavored."

Drawing a Line

The administration is presenting this change as a mere clarification meant to resolve legal ambiguity—as though Congress had simply misplaced a semicolon. Yet the Bush-era Office of Legal Counsel already rejected that argument in a 2008 opinion, concluding that the FBI had for years misread the "straightforward" language of the statute. And clarity is certainly needed, as it is hard to know just what falls under "categories of information parallel to subscriber information and toll billing records." The standard reference for lawyers in this sphere, David Kris's *National Security Investigations and Prosecutions*, simply notes that the scope of NSLs as applied to online activity is unclear. Even the Justice Department seems uncertain. In a 2001 response to congressional inquiries about the effect of the newly enacted PATRIOT Act, the Department Of Justice told Congress that "reasonable minds may differ" as to where the line should be drawn between addressing information equivalent to toll billing records and "content" requiring a search warrant.

Congress would be wise to specify in greater detail just what are the online equivalents of "toll billing records." But a blanket power to demand "transactional information" without a court order would plainly expose a vast range of far more detailed and sensitive information than those old toll records ever provided.

Consider that the definition of "electronic communications service providers" doesn't just include ISPs [Internet service providers] and phone companies like Verizon or Comcast. It covers a huge range of online services, from search engines and Webmail hosts like Google, to social-networking and dating sites like Facebook and Match.com to news and activism sites like RedState and Daily Kos to online vendors like Amazon and Ebay, and possibly even cafes like Starbucks that provide WiFi access to customers. And "transactional records" potentially covers a far broader range of data than logs of e-mail addresses or websites visited, arguably extending to highly granular records of the data packets sent and received by individual users.

As the Electronic Frontier Foundation has argued, such broad authority would not only raise enormous privacy concerns but have profound implications for First Amendment speech and association interests. Consider, for instance, the implications of a request for logs revealing every visitor to a political site such as Indymedia. The constitutionally protected right to anonymous speech would be gutted for all but the most technically savvy users if chat-forum participants and blog authors could be identified at the discretion of the FBI, without the involvement of a judge.

Data-Mining Technology

The right of "expressive association," which a unanimous Supreme Court similarly found to enjoy constitutional protection, would be equally imperiled. Though, the Court previously held that the government could not force politically controversial groups like the NAACP [National Association for the Advancement of Colored People] to reveal their membership rosters without judicial process. But as legal scholar Katherine Strandburg has argued, data-mining technology now holds out the temptation that just such patterns of "expressive association" can be revealed by sophisticated analysis of communications patterns and social-network ties—and perhaps even patterns of physical movement, as could be in-

---

Number of National Security Letters Requested, 2003–2006

	2003	2004	2005	2006
Non-U.S. Persons	10,232	8,494	8,536	8,605
U.S. Persons	6,519	8,943	9,475	11,517

TAKEN FROM: Office of the Inspector General, U.S. Department of Justice, "A Review of the FBI's Use of National Security Letters: Assessment of Corrective Actions and Examination of NSL Usage in 2006," United States Department of Justice website, March 2008, p. 10.

---

ferred from records of location-sensitive mobile devices. And when the goal is to detect the patterns of previously unidentified terrorists, such analysis requires vacuuming up the records of huge numbers of innocent persons, more or less by definition.

Moreover, the distinction between "content" and merely "transactional" information is not nearly as sharp as might be supposed. Certain communications protocols, for instance, transmit each keystroke a user makes in real time as a separate data "packet." Given the known regularities of the English language, standard keyboards, and human hands, it is theoretically possible to infer the content of a communication from a sufficiently precise record of packet transmission timing. While such an attack would probably be infeasible given current technologies and record-keeping practices, the legal change proposed by the FBI would not be limited to present technologies or practices.

More practically, consider records of keyword-sensitive targeted advertising delivered to users of Webmail services like Gmail, which could indirectly hint at the contents of the e-mail that triggered a specific ad. Or again, consider downloaded movies. Under the Video Privacy Protection Act of 1988, records of a customer's video-rental history are private and protected by law. But even if subscriber viewing histories using services like iTunes or Netflix were considered out of bounds, that history could be reconstructed from transaction logs showing the precise size of a user download. The examples are hypothetical—what matters is the more general point: An abstract distinction between metadata and "content" gives us no way of predicting the extent of highly intimate information that might be extracted as technology changes and the analytic tools of investigators become more sophisticated.

We increasingly live online. We flirt, shop, read, speak out, and organize in a virtual space where nearly every action leaves a digital trace—and where those breadcrumb bits often track us through the physical world as well. If the Obama administration gets its way, an agency that has already proved itself utterly unable to respect the limits of its authority will have discretion to map our digital lives in potentially astonishing detail, with no judge looking over their shoulders. That the administration and the FBI would seek such power under the guise of a "technical clarification" is proof enough that they cannot be trusted with it.

> "The FBI's senior leadership is committed to correcting the serious deficiencies in the FBI's use of [National Security Letters."

The FBI Is Committed to Ending Abuse of Its National Security Powers

Office of the Inspector General, Department of Justice

The Office of the Inspector General (OIG) at the Department of Justice (DOJ) conducts investigations and audits in order to prevent waste, fraud, and abuse at the DOJ. In the following viewpoint, the OIG states that the FBI has made numerous efforts to improve its handling of national security letters (NSLs). For example, it has put in place new data systems and more training for agents in the proper use of NSLs. Though the OIG reports some continued NSL abuses, it notes that the FBI has been responsive to criticism and is committed to further improvements.

As you read, consider the following questions:

1. When was the OIG's first report on the FBI's use of NSLs, and what time period did it cover?

Office of the Inspector General, Department of Justice, "A Review of the FBI's Use of National Security Letters: Assessment of Corrective Actions and Examination of NSL Usage in 2006," March 2008.

2. What office did the FBI create to make sure that NSLs were used correctly, and what did it model this office on, according to the author?

3. Why does the OIG say that it is too early to definitively state whether the new systems and controls developed by the FBI will eliminate all problems with NSLs?

The *USA PATRIOT Improvement and Reauthorization Act of 2005* (Patriot Reauthorization Act or the Act) directed the Department of Justice (Department or DOJ) Office of the Inspector General (OIG) to review, among other things, "the effectiveness and use, including any improper or illegal use, of national security letters[1] issued by the Department of Justice." The Act required the OIG to conduct reviews on the Federal Bureau of Investigation's (FBI) use of national security letters (NSL) for two separate time periods.

The OIG's first report on the FBI's use of NSLs, issued on March 9, 2007, covered calendar years 2003 through 2005. This is the OIG's second report on the FBI's use of NSLs. In this report we describe and assess the response by the FBI and the Department to the serious misuse of NSL authorities that our first report described. . . .

The FBI Has Made Progress

Our review concluded that, since issuance of our March 2007 report, the FBI and the Department have made significant progress in implementing the recommendations from that report and in adopting other corrective actions to address serious problems we identified in the use of national security letters. The FBI has also devoted significant energy, time, and resources toward ensuring that its field managers and agents understand the seriousness of the FBI's shortcomings in its use of NSLs and their responsibility for correcting these deficiencies.

1. A national security letter is used by the FBI to demand records or data from an individual or organization.

Our interviews of senior FBI officials, including the Director, the Deputy Director, and the General Counsel, indicate that the FBI's senior leadership is committed to correcting the serious deficiencies in the FBI's use of NSLs identified in our first report. They have attempted to reinforce throughout all levels of the FBI the necessity of adhering to the rules governing the use of NSL authorities.

For example, among other measures the FBI has issued needed guidance on the use of NSLs, provided mandatory training to FBI employees on the proper use of NSLs, and developed a new data system to facilitate the issuance of NSLs and improve the accuracy of NSL data in required congressional reports. The FBI has issued numerous NSL policies and guidance memoranda on topics that include the proper usage of NSLs and statutory and procedural authorizations and restrictions; a prohibition on use of exigent letters; the requirement for sufficient and independent supervisory and legal reviews; and the procedures for identifying and reporting possible intelligence violations.

The FBI has also created a new Office of Integrity and Compliance (OIC), modeled after private sector compliance programs, to ensure that national security investigations and other FBI activities are conducted in a manner consistent with appropriate laws, regulations, and policies. We believe this office can perform a valuable function by providing a process for identifying compliance requirements and risks, assessing existing control mechanisms, and developing and implementing better controls to ensure proper use of NSLs. However, we recommend that the FBI consider providing the OIC with a larger permanent staffing level so that it can develop the skills, knowledge, and independence to lead or directly carry out the critical elements of this new compliance program.

In addition to the FBI's efforts to address the OIG's recommendations, the Department's National Security Division (NSD) has implemented additional measures to promote better compliance with NSL authorities and to address other issues raised by our first report. For example, in 2007 the NSD began reviews to examine whether the FBI is using various intelligence techniques, including NSLs, in accordance with applicable laws, guidelines, and policies.

Committed to Additional Improvements

Also, the Department's Office of the Chief Privacy and Civil Liberties Officer and the Civil Liberties Protection Officer of the Office of the Director of National Intelligence convened a working group to examine how NSL-derived information is used and retained by the FBI, with special emphasis on the protection of privacy interests, and in August 2007 sent a report and proposal to the Attorney General on minimization procedures with respect to NSL-derived data. However, after review of this proposal, we concluded that the NSL Working Group's report did not adequately address measures to label or tag NSL-derived information and to minimize the retention and dissemination of such information. In February 2008, the Acting Chief Privacy and Civil Liberties Officer told us that the proposal had been withdrawn and that he intends to reconvene the NSL Working Group to reconsider the August 2007 report and proposal. . . .

The FBI's reviews confirmed that the types of deficiencies identified in our first NSL report had occurred throughout the FBI from 2003 through 2006. The FBI's field review was important because it covered a larger, statistically valid sample of NSLs and case files. The FBI reviews confirmed similar types of possible intelligence violations in the FBI's use of NSLs that we found. However, the FBI's field review found a higher overall possible IOB [Intelligence Oversight Board] violation rate (9.43 percent) than the OIG found (7.5 percent) in the sample we examined in our first NSL report.

However, we examined in detail the FBI's field review and determined that it did not capture all NSL-related possible intelligence violations in the files it reviewed, and therefore did not provide a fully accurate baseline from which to measure future improvement in compliance with NSL authorities. For example, during our re-examination of case files that FBI inspectors determined had no NSL-related possible intelligence violations in three field offices, we identified 15 additional NSL-related possible intelligence violations. In addition, because FBI inspectors were unable to locate information provided in response to a significant number of NSLs chosen for review in its sample, the results of the FBI's field review likely understated the rate of possible intelligence violations.

In short, despite the significant challenges facing the FBI in eliminating fully shortcomings in its use of NSLs, we believe the FBI and the Department have evidenced a commitment to correcting the problems we found in our first NSL report and have made significant progress in addressing the need to improve compliance in the FBI's use of NSLs. However, because only 1 year has passed since the OIG's first NSL report was released and some measures are not fully implemented or tested, we believe it is too early to definitively state whether the new systems and controls developed by the FBI and the Department will eliminate fully the problems with NSLs that we identified. We believe the FBI must implement all of our recommendations in the first NSL report, demonstrate sustained commitment to the steps it has taken and committed to take to improve compliance, implement additional recommendations described in this second report, consider additional measures to enhance privacy protections for NSL-derived information, and remain vigilant in holding FBI personnel accountable for properly preparing and approving NSLs and for handling responsive records appropriately.

Periodical Bibliography

The following articles have been selected to supplement the diverse views presented in this chapter.

American Civil Liberties Union	"National Security Letters," November 30, 2005. www.aclu.org/national-security-technology-and-liberty/national-security-letters.
Jim Arkedis	"Restoring a Proper Balance on Surveillance," Democratic Leadership Council, November 26, 2007.
Eric Bland	"'Underwear Bomber' Could Not Have Blown Up Plane," *Discovery News*, March 10, 2010. http://news.discovery.com/tech/underwear-bomber-explosion-plane-test.html.
Art Keller	"Why Was Faisal Shahzad a Bad Bombmaker?" The Afpak Channel on Foreign Policy, May 14, 2010. http://afpak.foreignpolicy.com/posts/2010/05/14/bad_bombmakers.
Mark Mazzetti, Sabrina Tavernise, and Jack Healy	"Times Square Car Bomb Case Widens with Arrests in Two Countries," *New York Times*, May 5, 2010.
Andy McCarthy	"The National Security Letter Controversy," *National Review Online*, March 10, 2007. www.nationalreview.com/corner/138864/fbi-national-security-letter-controversy/andy-mccarthy.
Patrick B. Pexton	"Times Square Bomber: A New Type of Threat to the U.S. Homeland?" *National Security*, May 10, 2010.
James Risen and Eric Lichtblau	"Court Affirms Wiretapping Without Warrants," *New York Times*, January 15, 2009.
Russell Seitz	"Just Say No to Airport Paranoia," Reason.com, January 12, 2010.

Jacob Sullum   "Why Use a National Security Letter When You Have Post-It Notes?" *Reason*, January 20, 2010.

John Yoo   "Why We Endorsed Warrantless Wiretaps," *Wall Street Journal*, July 16, 2009.

OPPOSING
VIEWPOINTS®
SERIES

CHAPTER 3

What Impact Does the U.S. Intelligence Community Have on Foreign Affairs?

Chapter Preface

U.S. intelligence plays a central role in the wars in Afghanistan and Iraq, and in counterterrorism efforts in the broader Muslim world. The resources devoted to these regions, however, may be hurting U.S. intelligence goals in other areas.

One major area of concern is China. China has taken advantage of the U.S. focus on terrorism and Islamic militants in several ways. The most obvious of these is in China's treatment of a Muslim ethnic group called the Uighurs. The Uighurs are concentrated in the western Xinjiang region of China. The Chinese have been accused of human rights abuses and repression of the Uighurs in Xinjiang. They have imprisoned activists and severely restricted religious and cultural activities. In July 2009, ethnic violence broke out in the region, with 150 people killed. China has justified its repressive actions by accusing Uighurs "of receiving training and indoctrination from Islamic militants in neighbouring Afghanistan, although little public evidence has been produced in support of these claims," according to a 2009 article on BBC News Online.

U.S. intelligence gathering in China has also suffered in recent years, according to some commentators. Joel Brenner, a top counter-intelligence officer, noted that "Iraq and the struggle with terrorism are sucking resources across the board," as quoted in a 2007 Bloomberg news article. The same article states that because U.S. intelligence is stretched thin, "China has systematically managed to gain sensitive information on U.S. nuclear bombs and ships and missile designs."

While some see China as a growing threat, others believe that China is not necessarily the highest priority for counter-intelligence activities. In a 2010 article in the *Washington Times*, Bill Gertz reported that "the White House National Security Council recently directed U.S. spy agencies to lower the priority placed on intelligence collection for China." Some intelligence officials were concerned that downgrading the priority level would make it harder to gather intelligence from China; however, Gertz said that administration officials explained off the record that the change was "part of the [Barack] Obama administration's larger effort to develop a more cooperative relationship with Beijing."

The following viewpoints examine other areas in which the U.S. intelligence priorities and strategies have affected or been involved in foreign policy decisions.

"The [Iraqi Survey Group] Report ... that has been used by one side of the debate as proof that Saddam had no [weapons of mass destruction] capability actually says quite the opposite."

Intelligence Justified the War in Iraq

James Lacey

James Lacey is a Washington, D.C.–based writer who focuses on defense and foreign-policy issues. In the following viewpoint, he argues that before the Iraq war in 2003, Iraqi dictator Saddam Hussein was in the process of creating weapons of mass destruction (WMD). Lacey argues that Saddam had the capacity to manufacture biological and chemical weapons and ballistic missiles and that he was working on developing nuclear weapons. Further, Lacey says that Saddam had plans to use these weapons against regional neighbors like Saudi Arabia and Israel. Lacey concludes that the invasion of Iraq in 2003 prevented the possible devastating deployment of WMD by Iraq.

As you read, consider the following questions:

1. Who does Lacey identify as "Dr. Germ," and how did she get that nickname?

2. Why does the author say it would be sheer folly to allow Saddam Hussein's regime to possess even the smallest amount of smallpox?

3. How long does Lacey say it would have taken Saddam Hussein to reconstitute bioweapons programs once he had escaped the sanctions regime?

For almost three years [2003–2006], the anti-war protesters have kept up the drumbeat: "Bush lied and people died." Because weapons of mass destruction (WMD) were not found in Iraq, an endless stream of commentators continues to declare that [Iraqi dictator] Saddam Hussein was not the serious threat the [George W. Bush] administration claimed him to be. The critics usually go even further, and assert that sanctions and the destruction of WMD facilities by U.N. investigators had done so much damage to WMD infrastructure that it would have taken Saddam years to rebuild it even to a minimal capacity.

The ISG Shows Saddam Was a Threat

But these claims ignore huge amounts of contrary evidence; and most of this evidence can be found in the final report of the Iraqi Survey Group (ISG)—the very same report that many critics hold up as proof positive that Iraq was not a WMD threat. The evidence found by the ISG (an investigative commission set up by the Bush administration after the invasion of Iraq) confirms that Saddam was preparing to rapidly reconstitute his WMD program the moment he broke out of sanctions, which—given the frayed state of the coalition against him—would inevitably have happened. Not only did Bush not "lie"; the critics themselves are guilty of selectively citing evidence and of ignoring facts inconvenient to their argument. The ISG report, as well as the other evidence that continues to come to light, demonstrates that Saddam couldn't be trusted with the apparatus of a modern state, which he would have turned quickly back to producing WMD as soon as circumstances allowed.

Consider just one datum: According to the report, Saddam had the capability to start anthrax [a bacteriological weapon] production within one week of making the decision to do so, and thereafter to produce *over ten tons* of weaponized anthrax a year. If even 1 percent of that amount—200 pounds—were released into the air over Washington, D.C., Congress's Office of Technology Assessment estimates that up to 3 million people would die.

How did Saddam keep such a massive capability from being discovered by the inspectors? Simply by hiding it in plain sight. For instance, at a facility called al-Hakam, Dr. Rihab Rashid Taha al-Azawi maintained a production line that produced ten tons of biopesticides for agricultural use each year. These biopesticides were produced in powder form and milled to 1 to 10 microns in size—but bio agents milled this finely are absolutely useless for agricultural purposes. Farmers found the biopesticide Dr. Rihab was sending them almost impossible to use, as it had to be hand-dropped one plant at a time or it would disappear. When they followed her recommendation to mix it with water and spray it, all they got was a thick slurry that clogged spray nozzles.

Though such finely milled powder may be useless for agricultural work, it is the perfect size for an inhalation bioweapon. (To be effective, anthrax must be milled at less then 10 microns.) Experts estimate that weaponized-anthrax spores that infect the skin will kill 50 percent of untreated patients; inhaled anthrax will kill 100 percent of untreated victims and 50 percent of those receiving immediate treatment. Simulations prior to Desert Storm [coalition forces sent against Iraq in 1991] estimated that an anthrax attack would kill over 25 percent of Coalition forces, as many as 200,000 men. In the hands of terrorists, this would be a weapon of incalculable value.

Iraq Was Developing Biological Weapons

Dr. Rihab, the supposed agricultural scientist, is better known to U.S. intelligence agencies as "Dr. Germ," the head of Saddam's biological-warfare [BW] program for most of the decade immediately preceding the invasion. A 1999 Defense Intelligence Agency [DIA] report called her the most dangerous woman in the world, and others have testified that she used political prisoners to test her bioweapons when she began to doubt she was getting accurate data from infected donkeys and dogs. When questioned by U.N. inspectors about al-Hakam, she claimed it was a chicken-feed plant. (Charles Duelfer, deputy executive chairman for the U.N. inspection team, later told reporters, "There were a few things that were peculiar about this animal-feed production plant, beginning with the extensive air defenses surrounding it.") According to the 1999 DIA report, the normally mild-mannered Rihab exploded into violent rages when questioned about al-Hakam, shouting, screaming, and, on one occasion, storming out of the room, before returning and smashing a chair.

In 1995, the U.N. inspectors showed Rihab documents obtained from the Israelis that demonstrated that Iraq had purchased ten tons of growth media from a British company called Oxoid. Shown this evidence, Rihab admitted to the inspectors that she had grown 19,000 liters of botulism toxin; 8,000 liters of anthrax; 2,000 liters of aflatoxins, which can cause liver cancer; clostridium perfringens, a bacterium that can cause gas gangrene; and ricin, a castor-bean derivative that can kill by impeding circulation. She also admitted conducting research into cholera, salmonella, foot-and-mouth disease, and camel pox. Neither the U.N. nor later inspectors were able to certify that all of this lethal cornucopia was ever destroyed.

Mobile Biological Weapons Labs

The ISG report dedicates an entire annex—20 pages of exhaustive analysis—to proving that the two suspected mobile bio-labs were not what Secretary of State Colin Powell claimed they were, before the U.N., in the run-up to war. But the report gives the discovery of Iraq's *actual* mobile bioweapons labs only a little over one page of attention.

After the 1995 defection of Saddam's son-in-law forced Iraq to admit to an extensive bioweapons program that it had been hiding, U.N. inspectors made an effort to eliminate it. But Saddam was not ready to give up all he had gained, and large portions of the bioweapons research program were continued in small mobile labs by a band of key scientists and technicians under the auspices of the Iraqi Intelligence Service. The ISG report says its investigators were unsure if any of this continuing bioweapons research was military-related. (No one ever bothered to ask the investigators if there was any *other* conceivable purpose for bioweapons.)

The ISG found evidence that at least five mobile bioweapons research labs were operating in Baghdad right up to the commencement of the Coalition invasion. At one site, which building residents claimed was a biological lab, investigators found chemicals, along with documents from lab employees asking for hazardous-duty pay for having to work with biological materials. Another lab, discovered in a Baghdad mosque, was filled with equipment belonging to a known bioweapons scientist. Still another clandestine lab was identified by the ISG team at the Baghdad Central Public Health Laboratory, which employees admitted was operated by the Intelligence Service for several years prior to 2003.

According to the ISG report, Samarra Drug Industries had tanks available for bio-agent production ranging from 100 to 10,000 liters that could have begun bioweapons production three to four weeks after the order was given. Just one of these 10,000-liter tanks, if filled with botulinum toxin, would be enough to wipe out the global population more than twice over.

Smallpox

And it could be worse: Even a thimbleful of smallpox [a highly contagious infectious disease that has been eradicated worldwide] germs would kill tens of millions. If smallpox were released by terrorists in the United States, where inoculations ceased in 1972, the result would be a disaster of almost unimaginable magnitude. With some estimates claiming that each infected person can infect between 10 and 17 others, the smallpox germ is the bioweapon of choice for terrorists. Given Saddam's close links to terror groups it would have been sheer folly to allow his regime to possess even the smallest capability to produce the germ.

The report states that the ISG found evidence that Iraq had in fact obtained smallpox cultures from the former Soviet Union in 1992. An Iraqi scientist also described for the ISG Iraq's efforts to develop smallpox for biological warfare by using eggs and viral cultures. ISG investigators visited two labs where they found equipment that appeared to be used for making animal vaccines, but "this dual-use equipment was assessed to be easily diverted to produce smallpox or other pathogenic viruses." The ISG also visited a location where animal pox vaccines were produced in tissue culture; its assessment was that this equipment could be used for the rapid production of large amounts of smallpox virus.

The ISG report states in bold font that investigators "uncovered no evidence to support smallpox R&D [research and development] at ASVI [Al-Amiriyah Serum and Vaccine Institute] for possible use as an offensive BW agent." Since this was the only facility in Iraq previously known to be associated with smallpox, the ISG's declaration that no bio-warfare research was being conducted there would seem to give the institute a clear bill of health. But the report also says that Dr. Rihab (a.k.a. Dr. Germ) made frequent visits to the institute to conduct unidentified biological-warfare research, and that the institute maintained a "small capability" for organic production; it needs to be stressed that when it comes to smallpox, you need only a very small amount to cause a catastrophic amount of damage.

Quick Development of WMDs

The question remains as to how long it would have taken Saddam to reconstitute WMD programs once he had escaped the sanctions regime. We have already seen the answer, in the case of bioweapons: a matter of weeks. For the rest of his programs, estimates vary. Tariq Aziz said recently that "Saddam would have restarted his WMD programs, beginning with the nuclear program, after sanctions." Aziz estimated that Iraq would have a full WMD capability two years after sanctions ended. Saddam's minister of military industrialization, Abdullah Mullah al-Huwaysh, told the ISG that Saddam would have reconstituted all of the proscribed programs within five years: This would have included having a sizeable nuclear inventory on hand for immediate use. Huwaysh also stated that in response to a Saddam inquiry regarding how long it would take to start mass production of chemical weapons, he told the dictator that mustard-gas production could start within six months, but Sarin and VX [both chemical agents used as weapons] would take a bit longer. Other WMD scientists claimed they had the materials and equipment to start mustard production in days, though such a fast start could damage the production equipment. By 2002, Iraq was already purchasing the precursor chemicals for the production of Sarin.

The ISG report quotes one senior official as stating that by successfully targeting scientists from Russia, Belarus, Bulgaria, Yugoslavia, China, and several other countries, and coupling them with resident know-how, Saddam ensured that he could rebuild his entire WMD program within two years.

After 1991, Iraq's own resident WMD scientists were moved from government labs into universities: There they could carry out their work without fear of being targeted by Coalition aircraft or much bothered by U.N. inspectors. According to the ISG report, "Saddam used the Ministry of Higher Education and Scientific Research through its universities to maintain, develop, and acquire expertise, to advance or preserve existent research projects and developments, and to procure goods prohibited by U.N. sanctions." By 1997, the number of university instructors working on WMD-related projects increased from a handful to 3,300, while a further 700–800 were sent to WMD-related companies on a regular basis to help with technical problems.

As the billions in Oil for Food cash flowed in, Saddam "began investing his growing reserves of hard currency in his military-industrial complex, increasing access to dual-use items and materials, and creating numerous research and development programs." Between 1996 and 2002, the annual budget for the military-industrialization ministry—which was responsible for WMD development—increased over forty-fold; by the time the Coalition invaded, it had grown to 1 trillion Iraqi dinars. The military "technical research" projects at Iraqi universities had skyrocketed from about 40 projects in 1997 to 3,200; and the military-industrialization workforce had expanded by over 50 percent in just three years. Saddam's WMD program was ready to move into overdrive. Financial salvation led Saddam to start thinking again about nuclear weapons. In 1999 he met with his senior nuclear scientists and offered to provide them with whatever they needed, and immediately thereafter new funds began to flow to the Iraqi Atomic Energy

Commission (IAEC). In 2001, Saddam mandated a large budget increase for the IAEC and increased the salaries of nuclear scientists tenfold. He also directed the head of the IAEC to keep nuclear scientists together, and instituted new privileges for IAEC scientists, while also investing in numerous new projects. From 2001 onward, Saddam convened frequent meetings with the IAEC to highlight new achievements.

Saddam Had WMD Capability

While money flowed back into the nuclear project, Saddam also maintained an extensive ballistic-missile program. He had previously told his ministers that he did not consider ballistic missiles to be WMD and that he would never accept missile-range restrictions. In 2002, Iraq began serial production of the Al Samoud II, a ballistic missile that violated U.N. range limits: Test firings reached 183 miles (294 km). By the time the Coalition invaded, 76 of these missiles had been produced and more were in the pipeline. Saddam also, in early 2002, directed the design and production of a missile with a range of 650 to 750 km, and told Huwaysh that he wanted it within six months. Huwaysh relates that when Saddam was informed that production would take longer, and that the twin Volga engines they could sneak through sanctions would reach only 550 km, he left the room "profoundly disappointed." The difference would keep Tel Aviv out of range. (These were not the only means Saddam pursued to strike at Israel: His al-Quds organization was building four UAVs—pilotless drones—that were to be turned over to Hamas [a Palestinian Islamist political and paramilitary organization] for the express purpose of killing Israeli prime minister Ariel Sharon.)

What becomes clear, as example piles upon example in the ISG Report, is that this document that has been used by one side of the debate as proof that Saddam had no WMD capability actually says quite the opposite. The fact that no weapons stockpiles were found in Iraq does not mean that Iraq was not a threat. According to the report, Saddam could start producing deadly bioweapons within a week of deciding to do it; he retained the capability to produce smallpox; he had the capability to start producing chemical weapons such as mustard gas within days or at most weeks of deciding to do so; he was actively preparing to produce the nerve agents Sarin and VX; he was pouring cash into nuclear research; he was working on his ballistic-missile program even as the Coalition crossed the border into Iraq.

In short, the unholy trinity of the WMD world—bioweapons, chemical weapons, and nuclear weapons—were either readily available or in the process of being created, along with the missiles required to deliver them anywhere in the region, when Coalition armor rolled into Baghdad [in 2003]. Three years later, we should still be very glad it did.

> "Lost in all the discussion about the
> lies and falsehoods used to justify this
> tragic war is the little-known determi-
> nation of top Bush administration
> officials to attack Iraq before the 9/11
> tragedy."

Intelligence Did Not Justify the War in Iraq

John F. McManus

John F. McManus is publisher of the New American *magazine and president of the John Birch Society. In the following view-point, McManus discusses an intelligence report that declared that there was never a connection between Iraqi dictator Sad-dam Hussein and the al Qaeda terrorist organization—a con-nection which the George W. Bush administration used as justi-fication for starting the 2003 war against Iraq. The author claims that the Bush administration intended to attack Iraq before the 9/11 tragedy and simply manipulated intelligence in order to justify its objective. Recent reports and books, McManus main-tains, are finally exposing the proof of falsehoods used to start the war on Iraq.*

John F. McManus, "Debunking Bush's Reason for War," *The New American*, October 16, 2006.

As you read, consider the following questions:

1. According to McManus, what role did the Iraqi National Congress (IRC) play in the Bush administration's attack on Iraq?

2. As stated by the author, what was the purpose of the Project for the New American Century (PNAC) when it was founded in 1997?

3. According to McManus, what happened "a mere nine days after 9/11"?

The 400-page report released on September 8 [2006] by the Senate Intelligence Committee has emphatically declared that there never was any connection between Saddam Hussein and al-Qaeda. The Bush administration justified starting the March 2003 war against Iraq with strong protestations that the Iraq leader was in bed with the 9/11 terrorists. Over recent years, when the reputed direct links to [al-Qaeda leader] Osama bin Laden couldn't be demonstrated, Mr. Bush continued to insist that connections did exist by claiming as recently as August 21 [2006] that Saddam "had relations with Zarqawi," the al-Qaeda official slain in a U.S.-led raid last June.

Pointedly countering the administration's repeated protestations, the committee cited a 2005 CIA assertion that Iraq's government "did not have a relationship, harbor, or turn a blind eye toward Zarqawi and his associates." Further citing the CIA report, the Senate document stated that "Saddam Hussein was distrustful of al-Qaeda and viewed Islamic extremists as a threat to his regime, refusing all requests from al-Qaeda to provide material or operational support."

False Information

Referring additionally to false information being given the administration by the exile group Iraqi National Congress (IRC), the report noted that IRC partisans wanted to give the Bush administration some reasons to attack Iraq; therefore, they reported that Saddam's government had nuclear, chemical, and biological weaponry. The Bush administration continued funding the IRC, despite being warned as far back as 2002 that the group's information was unreliable.

As more Americans conclude that the war was a mistake and should be ended, members of the Bush administration, including the president, have sought to shift the reason for the conflict. Original claims that Saddam was involved in the 9/11 attack, that he was working with bin Laden's al-Qaeda, and that he was planning to use weapons of mass destruction have all evaporated. Now the war is being fought, we are told, to wipe out terrorism. But the tactics being employed have resulted in increasing the number of terrorists, not only among massive numbers of Iraqis angry about the widespread destruction of their nation, but also among Muslims worldwide who view the American action as a war against their religion.

Lost in all the discussion about the lies and falsehoods used to justify this tragic war is the little-known determination of top Bush administration officials to attack Iraq before the 9/11 tragedy. After having served together in previous administrations, Dick Cheney, Donald Rumsfeld, and several other Bush administration appointees launched the Project for the New American Century (PNAC) in 1997. Its megalomaniacal purpose: create a worldwide American empire as part of our nation's "global responsibilities" and begin to "challenge regimes hostile to our interests." In January 1998, PNAC leaders formally urged President [Bill] Clinton to attack Iraq. When he failed to do as they wanted, they sent letters in May 1998 to House and Senate leaders seeking the start of action against Saddam's regime. House and Senate leaders didn't follow PNAC directives either.

Once the 2000 election was settled and PNAC leaders Cheney, Rumsfeld, Wolfowitz, and others were in the highest posts of government, PNAC issued Rebuilding America's Defenses, which called for deploying U.S. forces all over the

The CIA Knew Iraq Had No WMDs

On Sept. 18, 2002, CIA director George Tenet briefed President [George W.] Bush in the Oval Office on top-secret intelligence that [Iraqi dictator] Saddam Hussein did not have weapons of mass destruction [WMD], according to two former senior CIA officers. Bush dismissed as worthless this information from the Iraqi foreign minister, a member of Saddam's inner circle, although it turned out to be accurate in every detail. Tenet never brought it up again.

Nor was the intelligence included in the National Intelligence Estimate of October 2002, which stated categorically that Iraq possessed WMD. No one in Congress was aware of the secret intelligence that Saddam had no WMD.

Sidney Blumenthal, Salon, *September 6, 2007.*

globe whether they were wanted or not. Immediately after the 9/11 attack, President Bush released a document entitled National Security Strategy of the United States of America, a virtual rewrite of the PNAC's Rebuilding America's Defenses. Then a mere nine days after 9/11, PNAC leader William Kristol and 36 of the group's members cosigned a letter to Mr. Bush calling for an attack on Saddam's regime "even if evidence does not link Iraq" to the attack.

Finding a Way to Attack Iraq

Paul O'Neill, who served the Bush administration as its first Secretary of the Treasury, stated in Ron Suskind's *The Price of Loyalty* that from the first day the Bush team took office in early 2001, "there was a conviction that Saddam Hussein was a bad person and that he needed to go." O'Neill added: "It was all about finding a way to do it. The president saying 'Go find me a way to do this.'" Seven months before the 9/11 attack, therefore, the war drums were beating in the White House. PNAC leaders were the drummers.

Early in 2003, before the March 19 commencement of the war, PNAC leader Kristol and coauthor Lawrence Kaplan issued a book-length document entitled *The War over Iraq: Saddam's Tyranny and America's Mission*. It not only focused on their desire to attack Iraq, it also called for the United States to engage in other wars as a way to shape the world as the PNAC gurus would have it.

It's helpful that the Senate Intelligence Committee has published some definitive proof about the lies and falsehoods used to start this war. But the behind-the-scenes goals of the PNAC-led Bush administration need airing as well.

> *"Interrogations now under way could produce significant intelligence about the [Taliban's] leadership, capabilities and military operations at a critical time."*

U.S. Intelligence Has Had Successes Against the Taliban

Adam Entous and Sue Pleming

Adam Entous and Sue Pleming are both journalists working for the Reuters news agency. In the following viewpoint, they report that the Central Intelligence Agency (CIA) and Pakistani intelligence services (ISI) worked together to capture Mullah Baradar, one of the leaders of the Taliban. The Taliban is an Islamist group leading an insurgency in Afghanistan, Pakistan's neighbor. Entous and Pleming note that the joint raid may over time usher in further cooperation, which could be very helpful in the U.S. effort to stabilize Afghanistan and Pakistan and defeat the Taliban.

As you read, consider the following questions:

1. According to Entous and Pleming, what sort of intelligence do U.S. officials hope to get from interrogation of Mullah Baradar?

Adam Entous and Sue Pleming, "Taliban Chief's Capture Seen as Start, More Needed," Reuters, February 16, 2010. Reproduced by permission.

2. What do the authors say caused the CIA to step up drone attacks and intelligence-gathering operations in Pakistan?

3. Why is ISI cooperation with the CIA a highly sensitive issue in Pakistan, according to Entous and Pleming?

The capture of the Taliban's top military commander in Pakistan followed months of behind-the-scenes prodding by U.S. officials who saw inaction by Islamabad [the capital of Pakistan] as a major threat to their Afghan war strategy.

Increased Cooperation Is Possible

But officials and analysts said it was too soon to tell whether Pakistan's cooperation against Mullah Abdul Ghani Baradar—captured earlier this month [February 2010] in a joint raid in Karachi [Pakistan] by Pakistani and U.S. intelligence agencies—would be extended to other top militants on the U.S. hit list.

"This is a game of inches. It is highly unlikely the Pakistanis would turn 100 percent overnight," said former CIA analyst Bruce Riedel, now with the Brookings Institution, a Washington-based think tank.

Mullah Baradar has been described as one of the Afghan Taliban's top strategic leaders, and U.S. officials said interrogations now under way could produce significant intelligence about the group's leadership, capabilities and military operations at a critical time of stepped-up U.S. operations in neighboring Afghanistan.

"This is a major player in the Afghan Taliban. If he's off the streets, it would be a serious setback for the Taliban in the near term and deal a severe personal blow to (Taliban chief) Mullah Omar, who has relied on him for years as a trusted associate," a U.S. national security official said.

Other U.S officials were more cautious, citing the Taliban's resilience as an organization and ability to fill the void for leaders soon after they are captured or killed.

"How long it takes them to ... reconstitute depends on the situation," Colonel David Lapan, a Pentagon spokesman, said.

CIA Involvement in Raid

The raid that caught Mullah Baradar was carried out by Pakistan's spy agency, the Directorate for Inter-Services Intelligence, or ISI, and involved CIA operatives, according to U.S. officials who spoke on condition of anonymity.

It followed a year-long push led by U.S. National Security Adviser Jim Jones, Defense Secretary Robert Gates and Secretary of State Hillary Clinton to get Islamabad "off the fence" when it comes to reining in Afghan Taliban leaders who lead the insurgency from Pakistan, one official said.

White House spokesman Robert Gibbs pointed to increased cooperation and better intelligence sharing in recent months but declined to comment further, saying "this involves very sensitive intelligence matters."

"It's promising," another U.S. official said of the ISI's decision to mount the operation jointly with the CIA against Mullah Baradar. Asked where that cooperation would lead next, the official added: "We'll see."

Riedel, who led the [Barack] Obama administration's first review a year ago [2009] of Afghanistan and Pakistan strategy, largely attributed the shift to Islamabad coming around to the U.S. view that there are strong links between the Afghan and Pakistani Taliban.

"I heard from one Pakistani that the only good Taliban was a dead Taliban ... but will this lead to cooperation on all sides?—I would not go that far," said Riedel.

The CIA has stepped up unmanned aerial drone attacks and intelligence-gathering operations in Pakistan, particularly since a December 30 [2009] suicide bombing killed seven of the agency's employees at a U.S. base in eastern Afghanistan.

The successful joint raid targeting Mullah Baradar followed a drone strike in January [2010] that Pakistani and U.S. officials suspect killed Pakistani Taliban chief Hakimullah Mehsud.

Optimistic Amid Uncertainty

Lapan said General Stanley McChrystal, the commander of U.S. and NATO [North Atlantic Treaty Organization] forces in Afghanistan, has made clear he "considers the entire area, not just Afghanistan, as being part of the fight," underscoring Washington's call for Pakistan to help rein in the Taliban on both sides of the border.

In a visit to Pakistan last month, Gates warned of growing links between al Qaeda [the terrorist organization responsible for the September 11, 2001, attacks], the Taliban and Pakistan-based Lashkar-e-Taiba, the group accused of plotting the November 2008 attack in Mumbai [India, which left 173 dead and more than 300 wounded].

But U.S. officials held out little hope of a broader crackdown by Pakistan on the Taliban leadership council, which is said to be based in Quetta, on the heels of Mullah Baradar's capture, suggesting future raids would only come gradually as opportunities arise.

ISI cooperation with the CIA is a highly sensitive issue in Pakistan, where anti-American sentiment is high and conspiracy theories abound over what American spies and Special Operations forces are doing there and whether it infringes on the country's sovereignty.

Pakistan, for its part, has said it wants to play a bigger role in reconciliation efforts in Afghanistan and has told the United States this in recent months.

How Mullah Baradar's capture might fit into these talks is still unclear but U.S. military and political leaders have said repeatedly that the battle in Afghanistan will be won not only on the battlefield but in reconciling warring factions.

> *"Eight years into the war in Afghanistan, the U.S. intelligence community is only marginally relevant to the overall strategy."*

U.S. Intelligence Is Failing Against the Taliban

Michael T. Flynn, Matt Pottinger, and Paul D. Batchelor

Michael T. Flynn is a U.S. Army major-general and the top military intelligence officer in Afghanistan. Matt Pottinger serves as a company-grade officer. Paul D. Batchelor is a senior executive with the Defense Intelligence Agency. In the following viewpoint, they argue that intelligence services in Afghanistan are failing to provide useful information for the fight against the Taliban—the fundamentalist Islamist group leading the insurgency. They argue that intelligence agencies are focused on information about insurgents, when what is needed is general information about population, culture, and local conditions throughout Afghanistan. They say that without better intelligence, the United States will lose the fight against the Taliban.

As you read, consider the following questions:

1. What examples do the authors give of items that S-2 shops rarely gather, process, and write up assessments on?

2. According to Flynn, Pottinger, and Batchelor, what does merely killing insurgents result in?

3. What do the authors say is the difference between anti-insurgency and counterinsurgency?

Eight years into the war in Afghanistan, the U.S. intelligence community is only marginally relevant to the overall strategy. Having focused the overwhelming majority of its collection efforts and analytical brainpower on insurgent groups, the vast intelligence apparatus is unable to answer fundamental questions about the environment in which U.S. and allied forces operate and the people they seek to persuade. Ignorant of local economics and landowners, hazy about who the powerbrokers are and how they might be influenced, incurious about the correlations between various development projects and the levels of cooperation among villagers, and disengaged from people in the best position to find answers—whether aid workers or Afghan soldiers—U.S. intelligence officers and analysts can do little but shrug in response to high level decisionmakers seeking the knowledge, analysis, and information they need to wage a successful counterinsurgency.

Intelligence Failures at Every Level

This problem and its consequences exist at every level of the U.S. intelligence hierarchy, from ground operations up to headquarters in Kabul [the Afghan capital] and the United States. At the battalion level[1] and below, intelligence officers know a great deal about their local Afghan districts but are generally too understaffed to gather, store, disseminate, and digest the substantial body of crucial information that exists

1. The battalion is a military unit of between three hundred and thirteen hundred soldiers.

outside traditional intelligence channels. A battalion S-2 shop[2] will, as it should, carefully read and summarize classified human intelligence (HUMINT), signals intelligence (SIGINT), and significant activity (SIGACT) reports that describe improvised explosive device (IED) strikes and other violent incidents. These three types of reports deal primarily with the enemy and, as such, are necessary and appropriate elements of intelligence.

What lies beyond them is another issue. Lacking sufficient numbers of analysts and guidance from commanders, battalion S-2 shops rarely gather, process, and write up quality assessments on countless items, such as: census data and patrol debriefs; minutes from shuras [local council meetings] with local farmers and tribal leaders; after-action reports from civil affairs officers and Provincial Reconstruction Teams (PRTs); polling data and atmospherics reports from psychological operations and female engagement teams; and translated summaries of radio broadcasts that influence local farmers, not to mention the field observations of Afghan soldiers, United Nations officials, and non-governmental organizations (NGOs). This vast and underappreciated body of information, almost all of which is unclassified, admittedly offers few clues about where to find insurgents, but it does provide elements of even greater strategic importance—a map for leveraging popular support and marginalizing the insurgency itself.

The tendency to overemphasize detailed information about the enemy at the expense of the political, economic, and cultural environment that supports it becomes even more pronounced at the brigade [a unit composed of two–five battalions] and regional command levels. Understandably galled by IED strikes that are killing soldiers, these intelligence shops react by devoting most of their resources to finding the people who emplace such devices. Analysts painstakingly diagram in-

2. The battalion S-2 officer is in charge of gathering local intelligence.

surgent networks and recommend individuals who should be killed or captured. Aerial drones and other collection assets are tasked with scanning the countryside around the clock in the hope of spotting insurgents burying bombs or setting up ambushes. Again, these are fundamentally worthy objectives, but relying on them exclusively baits intelligence shops into reacting to enemy tactics at the expense of finding ways to strike at the very heart of the insurgency. These labor-intensive efforts, employed in isolation, fail to advance the war strategy and, as a result, expose more troops to danger over the long run. Overlooked amid these reactive intelligence efforts are two inescapable truths: 1) brigade and regional command analytic products, in their present form, tell ground units little they do not already know; and 2) lethal targeting alone will not help U.S. and allied forces win in Afghanistan.

Information on Population Is Needed

Speaking to the first point, enemy-centric and counter-IED reports published by higher commands are of little use to war-fighters in the field, most of whom already grasp who it is they are fighting and, in many cases, are the sources of the information in the reports in the first place. Some battalion S-2 officers say they acquire more information that is helpful by reading U.S. newspapers than through reviewing regional command intelligence summaries. Newspaper accounts, they point out, discuss more than the enemy and IEDs. What battalion S-2 officers want from higher-up intelligence shops are additional analysts, who would be more productive working at the battalion and company levels. The same applies to collection efforts. Officers in the field believe that the emphasis on force protection missions by spy planes and other non-HUMINT platforms should be balanced with collection and analysis of population-centric information. Is that desert road we're thinking of paving really the most heavily trafficked route? Which mosques and bazaars attract the most people from week to week? Is that local contractor actually implementing the irrigation project we paid him to put into service? These are the kinds of questions, beyond those concerning the enemy as such, which military and civilian decision-makers in the field need help answering. They elicit the information and solutions that foster the cooperation of local people who are far better than outsiders at spotting insurgents and their bombs and providing indications and warnings "left of boom" (before IEDs blow up).

The second inescapable truth asserts that merely killing insurgents usually serves to multiply enemies rather than subtract them. This counterintuitive dynamic is common in many guerrilla conflicts and is especially relevant in the revenge-prone Pashtun communities[3] whose cooperation military forces seek to earn and maintain. The Soviets [who invaded Afghanistan in 1979] experienced this reality in the 1980s, when despite killing hundreds of thousands of Afghans, they faced a larger insurgency near the end of the war than they did at the beginning. Given these two lessons, we must ask why, out of the hundreds of intel analysts working in brigade-level and regional command-level headquarters, only a miniscule fraction study governance, development, and local populations—all topics that must be understood in order to prevail. "Why the Intel Fusion Center can't give me data about the population is beyond me," remarked the operations officer of one U.S. task force, echoing a common complaint: "I don't want to say we're clueless, but we are. We're no more than fingernail deep in our understanding of the environment." If brigade and regional command intelligence sections were profit-oriented businesses, far too many would now be "belly up."

---

3. The Pashtuns are the ethnic group from which most Taliban insurgents are drawn.

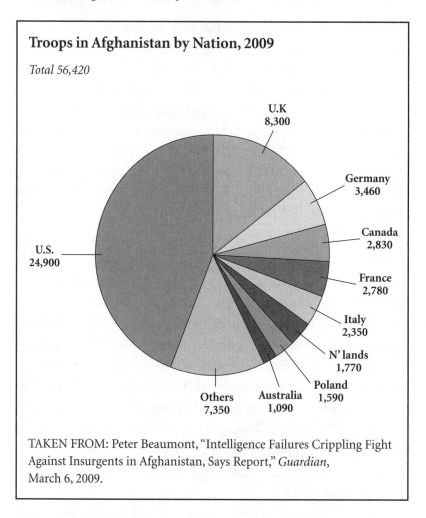

Troops in Afghanistan by Nation, 2009

Total 56,420

U.K
8,300

Germany
3,460

Canada
2,830

France
2,780

Italy
2,350

N' lands
1,770

Poland
1,590

U.S.
24,900

Others
7,350

Australia
1,090

TAKEN FROM: Peter Beaumont, "Intelligence Failures Crippling Fight Against Insurgents in Afghanistan, Says Report," *Guardian*, March 6, 2009.

Starved for Information

The next level up represents the top of the intel pyramid. Dozens of intelligence analysts in Kabul [capital of Afghanistan], along with hundreds more back in Tampa [Fla.], at the Pentagon, and throughout the Washington, D.C. area, are committed to answering critically important questions about the state of the conflict in Afghanistan and the impact of U.S. and allied military actions. They seek to respond to the queries posed by U.S. Forces-Afghanistan and ISAF [International Security Assistance Forces—the multinational force in Afghanistan] Commanding General Stanley McChrystal, Lieutenant General David M. Rodriguez of the ISAF Joint Command, and other decision-makers, up to and including the President of the United States. Their answers are essential to making informed strategic decisions.

The problem is that these analysts—the core of them bright, enthusiastic, and hungry—are starved for information from the field, so starved, in fact, that many say their jobs feel more like fortune telling than serious detective work. In a recent project ordered by the White House, analysts could barely scrape together enough information to formulate rudimentary assessments of pivotal Afghan districts. It is little wonder, then, that many decision-makers rely more upon newspapers than military intelligence to obtain "ground truth." While there is nothing wrong with utilizing credible information gathered by reporters, to restrict decision-makers so narrowly when deep and wide intelligence information is available shortchanges military personnel and needlessly jeopardizes the successful prosecution of the Afghanistan war.

Ironically, the barriers to maximizing available intelligence are surprisingly few. The deficit of data needed by high-level analysts does not arise from a lack of reporting in the field. There are literally terabytes of unclassified and classified information typed up at the grassroots level. Nor, remarkably, is the often-assumed unwillingness to share information the core of the problem. On the contrary, military officers and civilians working with ISAF allies, and even many NGOs [nongovernmental organizations such as humanitarian groups], are eager to exchange information. True, there are severe technological hurdles, such as the lack of a common database and digital network available to all partners, but they are not insurmountable.

The most salient problems are attitudinal, cultural, and human. The intelligence community's standard mode of operation is surprisingly passive about aggregating information that is not enemy-related and relaying it to decision-makers or fellow analysts further up the chain. It is a culture that is strangely oblivious of how little its analytical products, as they now exist, actually influence commanders.

It is also a culture that is emphatic about secrecy but regrettably less concerned about mission effectiveness. To quote General McChrystal in a recent meeting, "Our senior leaders—the Chairman of the Joint Chiefs of Staff, the Secretary of Defense, Congress, the President of the United States—are not getting the right information to make decisions with. We must get this right. The media is driving the issues. We need to build a process from the sensor all the way to the political decision makers." . . .

Anti-Insurgency vs. Counterinsurgency

The U.S. intelligence community has fallen into the trap of waging an anti-insurgency campaign rather than a counterinsurgency campaign. The difference is not academic. Capturing or killing key mid-level and high-level insurgents—anti-insurgency—is without question a necessary component of successful warfare, but far from sufficient for military success in Afghanistan. Anti-insurgent efforts are, in fact, a secondary task when compared to gaining and exploiting knowledge about the localized contexts of operation and the distinctions between the Taliban[4] and the rest of the Afghan population. There are more than enough analysts in Afghanistan. Too many are simply in the wrong places and assigned to the wrong jobs. It is time to prioritize U.S. intelligence efforts and bring them in line with the war's objectives.

---

4. The Taliban is the fundamentalist Islamist group leading the insurgency against the Afghan government and U.S. forces. The Taliban controlled Afghanistan in the late 1990s.

Doing so will require important cultural changes. Analysts must absorb information with the thoroughness of historians, organize it with the skill of librarians, and disseminate it with the zeal of journalists. They must embrace open-source, population-centric information as the lifeblood of their analytical work. They must open their doors to anyone who is willing to exchange information, including Afghans and NGOs as well as the U.S. military and its allies. As General Martin E. Dempsey, commander of the U.S. Army Training and Doctrine Command, recently stated, ". . . [T]he best information, the most important intelligence, and the context that provides the best understanding come from the bottom up, not from the top down."

Leaders must invest time and energy in selecting the best, most extroverted, and hungriest analysts to serve in Stability Operations Information Centers. These will be among the most challenging and rewarding jobs an analyst could tackle.

The Cold War notion that open-source [unclassified] information is second "class" is a dangerous, outmoded cliché. Lieutenant General Samuel V. Wilson, former director of the Defense Intelligence Agency, captured it perfectly: "Ninety percent of intelligence comes from open sources. The other 10 percent, the clandestine work, is just the more dramatic. The real intelligence hero is Sherlock Holmes, not James Bond."

Meaningful change will not occur until commanders at all levels take responsibility for intelligence. The way to do so is through devising and prioritizing smart, relevant questions—"information requirements"—about the environment as well as the enemy. Of critical importance to the war effort is how a commander orders his or her intelligence apparatus to undertake finite collection, production, and dissemination. "If a commander does not effectively define and prioritize intelligence requirements," Marine Corps doctrine warns, "the entire effort may falter."

In-Depth Analysis Is Needed

The format of intelligence products matters. Commanders who think PowerPoint storyboards and color-coded spreadsheets are adequate for describing the Afghan conflict and its complexities have some soul searching to do. Sufficient knowledge will not come from slides with little more text than a comic strip. Commanders must demand substantive written narratives and analyses from their intel shops and make the time to read them. There are no shortcuts. Microsoft Word [a text-based program], rather than PowerPoint [a graphics-based program], should be the tool of choice for intelligence professionals in a counterinsurgency.

Employing effective counterinsurgency methods is not an option but a necessity. General McChrystal routinely issues distinct orders and clear guidance on the subject. When he states, "The conflict will be won by persuading the population, not by destroying the enemy," it is not just a slogan, but an expression of his intent. Too much of the intelligence community is deaf to these directions—this must be remedied, and now. The General's message must resonate throughout the entire community—top to bottom.

Historical lessons run the risk of sounding portentous, but disregarding them comes at a high price. History is replete with examples of powerful military forces that lost wars to much weaker opponents because they were inattentive to nuances in their environment. A Russian general who fought for years in Afghanistan cited this as a primary reason for the Soviet Union's failures in the 1980s.

A single-minded obsession with IEDs, while understandable, is inexcusable if it causes commanders to fail to outsmart the insurgency and wrest away the initiative. "A military force, culturally programmed to respond conventionally (and predictably) to insurgent attacks, is akin to the bull that repeatedly charges a matador's cape—only to tire and eventually be defeated by a much weaker opponent," General McChrystal and U.S. Forces-Afghanistan Command Sergeant Major Michael T. Hall recently wrote. "This is predictable—the bull does what comes naturally. While a conventional approach is instinctive, that behavior is self-defeating."

The intelligence community—the brains behind the bullish might of military forces—seems much too mesmerized by the red of the Taliban's cape. If this does not change, success in Afghanistan will depend on the dubious premise that a bull will not tire as quickly as a Russian bear.

> *"The CIA . . . has repeatedly failed to warn the White House of looming threats."*

The CIA Has Failed to Advance U.S. Interests

John Judis

John Judis is senior editor at the New Republic *and a contributing editor at the* American Prospect. *In the following viewpoint, he argues that the Central Intelligence Agency (CIA) has historically provided poor intelligence, leading to dangerous international results. He says that the CIA's failures are due in large part to its culture of secrecy, which privileges bureaucratic groupthink and marginalizes information that runs contrary to the consensus. Further, Judis argues, the secrecy of the CIA has allowed it to serve as a private army for the president, advancing unpopular and dangerous policies. Judis concludes that the CIA should be abolished.*

As you read, consider the following questions:

1. What examples does Judis give of instances in which the CIA proved inept at analyzing current situations?

2. What countries have been targeted for overthrow by the CIA, according to the author?

3. According to Judis, Senator Moynihan proposed moving the CIA's functions into what department, and for what reason?

In early 2002 the CIA took custody of captured Al Qaeda [the terrorist organization responsible for the September 11, 2001, attacks] commander Ibn Shaykh Al Libi. The agency loaned him to the Egyptians whom, under torture, he told of extensive ties between Al Qaeda and Saddam Hussein's Iraq. The CIA reclaimed its prisoner and reported the Egyptians' findings to the White House, which used them to justify invading Iraq. Al Libi subsequently recanted, claiming his testimony had been coerced, and in March 2004, a year after American tanks rumbled into Baghdad [the capital of Iraq], the CIA withdrew its support for his assertions.

The CIA Should Not Have Been Created

In his memoir, *Present at the Creation,* former Secretary of State Dean Acheson expressed his misgivings about the creation of the CIA in 1947. "I had the gravest forebodings about this organization and warned the President that as set up neither he, the National Security Council, nor anyone else would be in a position to know what it was doing or to control it." In 1991 and again in 1995, Senator Daniel Patrick Moynihan introduced bills to abolish the CIA and assign its functions to the State Department, which is what Acheson and his predecessor, George Marshall, had advocated. But Moynihan's proposal was treated as evidence of his eccentricity rather than of his wisdom and never came to a vote.

It's time to reconsider Moynihan's proposal, or least the reasoning behind it. Al Libi's case, combining gross incompetence with the violation of international law, shows that the problems Moynihan and others cited have, if anything, gotten worse under [U.S. President] George W. Bush. The intelligence reform act passed last year [2004] didn't address them; and the current director Porter Goss appears oblivious to them. These problems have for years plagued the two main functions of the agency: intelligence gathering and covert action.

The CIA was established to prevent unanticipated disasters, such as the Japanese attack on Pearl Harbor, but it has repeatedly failed to warn the White House of looming threats. It missed the North Korean invasion of the South in 1950, and the Chinese entry into the war that fall; Israel, France, and Great Britain's attack on the Suez Canal and Egypt in 1956; the Soviet invasion of Czechoslovakia in 1968; the Shah of Iran's ouster in 1979; the Soviet invasion of Afghanistan that year; the Iraqi invasion of Kuwait in 1990; the Indian nuclear tests in 1998 ("We didn't have a clue," CIA director George Tenet remarked afterwards); the attack on the World Trade Center in 1993; the bombing of American military barracks in Saudi Arabia in 1996 and of U.S. embassies in Africa in 1998; the attack on the USS *Cole* in 2000; and of course the attack on the World Trade Center and Pentagon in September 2001.

The agency has been equally inept at analyzing current situations. The CIA consistently overestimated Soviet military and economic strength. In 1986 agency deputy director Robert Gates insisted to Secretary of State George Schultz, "The Soviet Union is a despotism that works." In the early 1960s the CIA wildly misjudged opposition in Cuba to Fidel Castro even in the face of public accounts to the contrary. In the late '80s it underestimated Saddam Hussein's chemical, biological, and nuclear weapons programs. From 1992 to 2004, it fueled illusions that Saddam still had these programs.

Faulty Intelligence Leads to Disasters

Of course, the CIA did get some things right. It predicted, for instance, the exact length of the Six Day War in 1967. But many of the things it got wrong had disastrous consequences. The failure of the Bay of Pigs invasion of Cuba in 1961, because of faulty CIA intelligence, led to the Cuban missile crisis the next year—probably the closest the United States and the Soviet Union got to a nuclear war. Mistaken intelligence during the Balkan war [1991–1995] led to American planes destroying the Chinese embassy in Belgrade. And the WMD [weapons of mass destruction] errors in Iraq justified a war that might otherwise not have taken place.

Then there is the CIA's record of covert action. The agency was initially designed to gather information—whether through analysis or spying. But in the early '50s, it took upon itself a new function: serving as a secret army to topple governments that were deemed hostile to American interests. The full list is not public, but countries targeted include Iran, Syria, Angola, Guatemala, Cuba, South Vietnam, Chile, Angola, Nicaragua, Panama, and, of course, Afghanistan and Iraq. Some of these efforts were initially successful, but they have often had unwelcome consequences. In 1978, for instance, the secular and Islamic forces that took over Iran cited CIA support for the coup in 1953 that restored the Shah to explain their hostility to the United States.

In almost all these cases—except, perhaps, during the reign of William Casey [director 1981–87 under President Ronald Reagan]—the CIA was acting under official White House supervision. And some of the CIA's intelligence failures can also be laid at the White House door. Without pressure from the vice president's office and the Pentagon, for instance, the CIA might not have validated the Bush administration's claims that Iraq possessed WMD.

A Culture of Secrecy

But as Moynihan argued in his last book, *Secrecy*, there is a way in which the CIA's peculiar structure and function has encouraged errors and magnified their importance. Moynihan

Torture and Assassination

In 2004, photographs from the [CIA-controlled] Abu Ghraib prison in Iraq [showing the torture of prisoners] were published, and they horrified Americans.... Denunciations of the [George W.] Bush administration were commonplace. But this was not an isolated thing.... It fit in with a pattern we had glimpses of thirty years earlier in congressional investigations of the CIA. In 1975, we learned about an American campaign of assassinations planned, abetted, encouraged, and sometimes accomplished. The CIA had at least *tried* to murder leaders around the world—General René Schneider of Chile, Rafael Trujillo of the Dominican Republic, Patrice Lumumba of the Congo, Zhou Enlai of China, the Diem brothers of Vietnam, Fidel Castro of Cuba.... These activities were even worse than the crimes committed at Abu Ghraib, since murder is worse than torture.

Garry Wills, Bomb Power: The Modern Presidency and the National Security State, *2010.*

described a "culture of secrecy" created by the CIA and other intelligence agencies. This culture produced a distinction between insiders and outsiders; and outsiders, no matter their experience or expertise, couldn't possibly know with the same degree of certainty as insiders what was going on in a foreign country. For instance, the CIA ignored an extensive poll taken in Cuba just prior to the Bay of Pigs invasion by political scientist Lloyd A. Free that demonstrated widespread support for Fidel Castro. And prior to the Iraq war, the agency insisted that U.N. inspectors who reported an absence of WMD were being duped by Iraqis.

The distinction between insiders and outsiders not only insulated CIA analysts from obvious questions that outsiders without security clearances might ask; it also bestowed a special status upon the findings that were produced. Their very secrecy made them appear more likely to be true. Moynihan recounted how government officials gave special credence to the Gaither Report, which in 1957 wrongly predicted Soviet economic and military superiority, because it was classified.

In such a culture, dissenters risk isolation and even losing their clearances. That, in turn, serves to reinforce conventional wisdom on any given topic. Former CIA Director Stansfield Turner's account of why the agency was wrong about the Soviet economy could easily apply to the agency's deliberations in 2002 over whether Iraq was importing aluminum tubes for making nuclear bombs. "If some individual CIA analysts were more prescient than the corporate view," Turner wrote, "their ideas were filtered out in the bureaucratic process; and it is the corporate view that counts because that is what reaches the president and his advisers."

The culture of secrecy also makes those at the top of intelligence agencies highly susceptible to political pressure from above. Without a public community to sustain contrary conclusions, they dare not risk defying the expectations of those at whose discretion they serve. Tenet appears to have been particularly eager to please his superiors—whether in insisting that the Al Shifa factory in Sudan made chemical weapons [the factory was bombed, many believe erroneously, in 1998] or declaring that proof of Iraqi WMD was a "slam dunk."

Finally, the culture of secrecy has created common ground between CIA directors who have sought a special niche for their organization and presidents who have wanted to undertake foreign policies that would violate domestic or international law. The CIA has functioned as the White House's secret army, which is not subject to the same scrutiny as the regular armed forces. The CIA has tried to assassinate foreign leaders, mined harbors, and, most recently, tortured prisoners. If Congress had openly debated these actions, they would not have been approved. Some eventually caused an international uproar that undermined the legitimacy of American foreign policy.

Moynihan certainly understood the problem; but what about his solution? He proposed moving the CIA's functions into the State Department, where they would be more subject to international law and congressional oversight. But questions about this proposal abound. Would the State Department also perform covert operations, and not simply spying, overseas? What would happen to the intelligence agencies within the Pentagon and to the National Security Agency (which under George W. Bush appears to have taken on some of the domestic spying functions that were denied the CIA after Watergate)? Who would oversee them? The answers to these questions are unclear. What is clear is that the CIA is broken. And to repair it, we may have to start from scratch.

> *"To blame [CIA] analysts for tailoring their work to fit what policymakers might think is acceptable or credible is unfair."*

The CIA Should Not Be Blamed for Policy Failures

Roger Z. George

Roger Z. George was a career intelligence officer at the Central Intelligence Agency (CIA) before becoming a professor at the National War College. In the following viewpoint, he discusses John M. Diamond's book The CIA and the Culture of Failure. *In the context of this book, George argues that the CIA should not be blamed for failing to predict important events such as the fall of the Soviet Union. Rather, he says that the job of analysts is to point out possibilities to policy makers. George concludes that blaming the CIA alone for poor policy results can imperil intelligence and national security.*

As you read, consider the following questions:

1. According to George, what did the CIA get right and what did it get wrong about the Soviet economy prior to the Soviet collapse?

Roger Z. George, "The CIA and the Culture of Failure: U.S. Intelligence from the End of the Cold War," *Studies in Intelligence*, April 21, 2009.

2. Why does the author say that the CIA did not focus on Iraq prior to the American invasion of Kuwait in 1990?

3. What did the CIA predict regarding Yugoslavia before 1990, and what effect did this prediction have on U.S. policy, according to George?

Rising above the "gotcha" or the "connect the dots" simplicity of the growing genre of "intelligence-failure" literature, John Diamond's *The CIA and the Culture of Failure* is one book of the genre worth reading if one is all you choose to read. While the title is off-putting and misleading, Diamond explains it early in a way that compelled this reviewer to see if the author could make his case. The former *Chicago Tribune* and *USA Today* reporter on national security asserts in his introduction that "failure refers not to alleged CIA incompetence, which, though it occurs in cases we will explore, is often overstated by the agency's critics." What he explores instead is the product of an "atmosphere of declining confidence in the abilities of U.S. intelligence to do its job." Hence, the fault lies not only in the Agency's performance but in US politics since the collapse of the Soviet Union began in 1989.

Struggling After the Fall of Communism

Diamond spent two years piecing together his story from information released in the Agency's declassification programs, congressional hearings, commission postmortems, policymaker memoirs, and interviews with former Agency officials. He does not attempt to cover the Agency's entire history or to deal with every issue or controversy in which CIA has been involved since 1991. He says very little, for example, about [intelligence] collection or covert operations. One exception is a chapter on Aldrich Ames [a CIA officer convicted of spying for Russia in 1994] in which Diamond tries to demonstrate how Ames put CIA "in Chapter 11," in the words of former Deputy Director of Central Intelligence John McLaughlin. In his many sources, he detects a steady decline in CIA's status and performance.

The book unfolds in a discussion of the CIA's analytic record on the fall of the Soviet Union [USSR], which Diamond links to later problems in CIA's analysis on terrorism and Iraq. Like other authors, he acknowledges the shock of the loss of CIA's main target and object of analysis, but unlike other Agency critics, he does not entirely blame the Agency for not predicting the USSR's fall. "In a sense," he writes, "the CIA set itself up for later failures of analysis by its occasionally prescient early 1980s assessments of the pressures toward radical change in the Soviet bloc." He credits CIA for forecasting the risks—including coup plotting—[Soviet leader] Mikhail Gorbachev ran in trying to right the sinking ship of socialism. However, the Agency never fully appreciated the centrifugal forces at play in Soviet society and consequently could not anticipate or appreciate the far-reaching proposals that Gorbachev was to lay down in the late 1980s.

Rather than leave it at that, Diamond makes an observation few other critics acknowledge, namely, that analysis is not just about prediction. As he puts it:

> The scorn heaped on the Agency in the early 1990s—scorn that had a significant and damaging impact on intelligence spending at what we now know was a critical time in the emergence of militant Islam—is based on the dubious assumption that predicting the breakup should have been an easy call.

The Soviet breakup, he notes, involved both a complicated set of events in that society and significant interactions with the United States. Hence, he believes that "getting it right in the case of the Soviet breakup, required foresight about shifts in U.S. and Soviet policy as well as the interaction between those shifts." Debates raged throughout the [U.S. president Ronald] Reagan era over the proper way to deal with, if not bring down, the Soviet Union. CIA's place, according to Diamond, "was somewhere in the middle." It wrote about structural economic flaws but consistently overestimated Soviet GNP [gross national product—a measure of an economy's size], it accurately gauged many Soviet military programs but undervalued the overall strain defense placed on the economy, and it identified the falling quality of life as a major threat to stability but never questioned Moscow's ability to control the pressures. Diamond asserts that CIA followed its natural instinct to find a middle course between hawks and doves. The result satisfied no one, and CIA lost its credibility. In the end, "neither the political left nor right in America had a particular interest in defending the CIA against the charge of intelligence failure."

September 11 and Iraq

This description of CIA's political plight after 1989 sets the stage for the chapters on 9/11 and the Iraq War. In them Diamond asserts that CIA analysis often tacked within the confines of a supercharged political environment in which every estimative misjudgment or mistaken analysis had its predictable and often over-compensating adjustment. In many cases, CIA was judged to be changing its analytic course, flipping assumptions on their heads, or learning the next lesson in a way that guaranteed a future failure. Diamond also notes that much of the fault for this zig-zagging is driven by the shifting priorities and preoccupations of the policymakers CIA serves. "Intelligence reporting, in no small degree, reflects less the views of analysts than the view implied by questions policymakers have asked those analysts to answer." So, if the first Bush administration [of President George H.W. Bush] showed no interest in Iraq prior to its invasion of Kuwait in 1990, CIA was prone not to focus on it or to develop good sources; likewise when "containment" was thought to be working against Iraq during the [President Bill] Clinton administration, there was little incentive for CIA to develop sources or focus on what was not known about [Iraqi capital] Baghdad's WMD [weapons of mass destruction] programs. Along the way, Diamond applauds CIA for getting many things right and for trying to warn inattentive policymakers.

Stepping back from the argument itself, Diamond's account of the CIA's post-1989 analytic record deftly describes the interaction of intelligence with policy, making it a far more sophisticated and well-sourced treatment than many published critiques. Even though the *Culture of Failure* does not presume to be comprehensive in examining the many issues CIA has had on its plate since 1989, those who actually worked on the issues will have to admire Diamond's attention to detail, his meticulous sequencing of events, and his placement of events into their political contexts. No doubt, practitioners aware of still-classified material will quibble with some details or inferences and conclusions, but most will still find the volume a handy update to Christopher Andrew's book, *For the President's Eyes Only*, which does not cover the Clinton and George W. Bush administrations.

A Culture of Failure

But does Diamond's core thesis, his quasi-deterministic view of CIA's "culture of failure," hold up on full reading? I am not convinced. First, like many books in the "failure" genre, this one suffers from hindsight bias. The author finds that certain events—once all the facts are known—seem so much clearer than they could have been at the time. No analyst, and perhaps only a few senior Intelligence Community managers, could possibly have had the "bigger picture" in mind when formulating hypotheses about the Soviet Union, [terrorist leader Osama] Bin Laden, or Iraq. Analysts stay in their lanes, and, for reasons of analytic integrity, tend not to put themselves in the policymakers' position of understanding how their analyses will affect policy or how their analyses will be perceived by a particular policymaker. To blame analysts for tailoring their work to fit what policymakers might think is acceptable or credible is unfair, attributing to them insight most are unlikely to have. In any case, the thesis cannot explain why CIA and the Intelligence Community could get the Iraq WMD story so wrong but got its assessments of an alleged al-Qaeda–Iraq linkage and a post-Saddam Iraq so right. Uneven analytic expertise and rigor is a likelier explanation.

Second, Diamond seems to imply that "lessons learned" from one analytic experience are transmitted seamlessly to other analytic units. His argument that the Agency's damaged reputation after the fall of the Berlin Wall haunted its terrorism analysis and later its analysis of Iraq WMD may sound plausible in the abstract, but is too simplistic. Very few analysts and managers who lived through the Reagan-era intelligence-policy disputes over the Soviet Union were working the terrorism or Iraq issues. So, somehow this "culture of failure" had to be transplanted in the younger generation of analysts who came to populate the DI [Directorate of Intelligence] in the 1990s. Yet, there is no evidence in the book that any terrorism analyst or weapons analyst had such lessons in mind when they examined their particular targets. Moreover, both in-house and outside critiques of the Agency's performance on the Iraq WMD issue fault analysts for not having learned earlier lessons—that is, they committed the same sort of cognitive errors made by earlier analysts during the Cuban Missile Crisis, the 1973 Middle East War, the 1979 Iran Revolution, and indeed the fall of the Soviet Union. So, how can Diamond conclude that a past era had such a dramatic impact on a more recent one?

Prediction Not the CIA's Only Role

Third, despite Diamond's claim that prediction is not the sole metric of the Agency's performance, virtually all of his book seems to focus on whether the Agency's forecasts were more correct than not. Again, this simplifies the role of analysis to a game of odds-making. Like other critics, he dismisses or plays down the role of uncertainty in the analytic process; that is, analysts often must warn policymakers less about the certainty of a bad outcome and more about the uncertainty surrounding any judgment about the future. This is unsatisfying for policymakers but essential if analysts are to provide objective and transparent judgments. If, in 1987, CIA had predicted the end of the Soviet Union by the end of the decade, would anyone have listened? Exactly such a prediction was made regarding the breakup of Yugoslavia in 1990—which he does not examine—and had almost no impact on the first Bush administration. Analytic certitude does not guarantee an impact on policy, but raising the possibility of deeper change, as CIA did in its many analyses of the Soviet Union, at least prepares policymakers to hedge bets in dealing with uncertain futures. Had Diamond considered this uncertainty factor, he might well have arrived at different conclusions regarding the agency's performance or continued relevance. Indeed, he might have shifted more responsibility to the policymakers' side of the score sheet.

Fourth and finally, one wishes a seasoned journalist who has followed national security and intelligence policy for more than 20 years would have made an effort to address the media's contribution to the post-9/11 political environment. Was not the media part of the zeitgeist in which CIA became the whipping boy for failed policies? And in his discussion of the Iraq WMD story, should Diamond not have at least mentioned how readily prominent journalists bought into the mindset that Saddam had WMD and was cleverer than we all thought? If he is correct in arguing that analysts felt the burden of declining credibility over the years since 1989, at least part of that culture of failure was being transmitted by a press that found it appealing to focus on the Agency's failings more than its successes. Unlike this book, which acknowledges the difficulty of assessing the full record, the media have painted intelligence in black and white—either tainted by potiticization or irrelevant to critical national decisions, when the truth lies elsewhere.

Despite these flaws, the book makes an important contribution by highlighting the inherently inseparable nature of policy and the intelligence work behind it. Neither operates in a vacuum, and policymakers and intelligence officers work better when they understand and acknowledge the impact they have on each other. Wisely, Diamond states, "there is no bright line between success and failure, no column of intelligence activities on one side labeled 'successes' and another on the other side labeled 'failures.'" Thankfully, Diamond offers no over-simplified silver bullet as a solution to this intelligence-policy problem. Nor does he offer much hope for improvement for the future. Indeed, he acknowledges that the themes he examines—"the politicization of intelligence, the error-prone nature of the business, the tendency of bureaucracies to stumble into new kinds of failure while striving to avoid repeating past mistakes"—are not unique to the period after the Soviet Union or to intelligence. More somberly, he sees and expects the gap between policy and intelligence to widen. In providing this judgment, he performs the useful function of cautioning future administrations that they need to work on making this relationship as transparent and collaborative as possible. His message is that using the CIA to justify future actions, or excuse past mistakes, inevitably makes the Agency less effective and ultimately can undermine the nation's security.

Periodical Bibliography

The following articles have been selected to supplement the diverse views presented in this chapter.

Martin Evans	"US Military Chief Brands Afghan Intelligence Mission 'Clueless,'" *Daily Telegraph* (London), January 5, 2010.
Helen Fessenden and Jon Kyl	"Iraq: Intelligence, Facts, and Fantasies," Council on Foreign Relations, March 12, 2004. www.cfr.org/publication/6861/iraq.html?id=6861.
Melvin Goodman	"The Corruption of Intelligence in the Leadup to the Invasion of Iraq," Center for International Policy, June 2006. www.cfr.org/publication/6861/iraq.html?id=6861.
Margaret Henoch	"Why Congress & the CIA Clash, and Why That Hurts National Security," *U.S. News & World Report*, August 3, 2009. http://politics.usnews.com/opinion/articles/2009/08/03/why-congress-and-the-cia-clash-and-why-that-hurts-national-security.html.
Christopher Hitchens	"Abolish the CIA," *Slate*, December 10, 2007. www.slate.com/id/2179593/.
Zachary Karabell	"Two Agents, Two Paths: How the CIA Became a Vital Operation," *Foreign Affairs*, July/August 2003.
Mark Mazzetti and Scott Shane	"Senate Panel Accuses Bush of Iraq Exaggerations," *Washington Post*, June 5, 2008.
Richard Norton-Taylor	"Our Afghan Intelligence Failure," *Guardian* (Manchester, UK), January 5, 2010.
Paul R. Pillar	"Intelligence, Policy, and the War in Iraq," *Foreign Affairs*, March/April 2006.
Walter Pincus	"Analysts Behind Iraq Intelligence Were Rewarded," *Washington Post*, May 28, 2005.
Sayed Salahuddin	"Pakistan to Hand over Taliban Leader to Afghanistan," *National Post*, February 24, 2010.

CHAPTER 4

What Role Should Torture Play in U.S. Intelligence?

Chapter Preface

Extraordinary rendition is a term used to describe the extra-judicial, often clandestine, transfer of a person from one state to another. Under the George W. Bush administration, the United States transferred some terrorist suspects to other countries with the knowledge, and even the expectation, that the suspects would be tortured for information. The American Civil Liberties Union, in a 2005 article, said that some of these suspects were subjected to "waterboarding, electrocutions, beatings, extreme isolation, and psychological torture."

Some commentators have defended extraordinary rendition as a necessary security measure. Writing in a 2008 article in the *New York Times*, Reuel Marc Gerecht argued that "if the choice is between non-deniable aggressive questioning conducted by Americans and deniable torturous interrogations by foreigners acting on behalf of the United States," then the latter is preferable. Barack Obama, who opposed torture when he ran for president in 2008, backed the continuation of the extraordinary rendition program after he entered office. Obama pledged to regulate the program more carefully to ensure that suspects were not tortured, according to a 2009 *New York Times* article by David Johnston. However, many human rights organizations argued that there was no way to assure that suspects would not be tortured once they were handed over to foreign governments.

Some commentators have argued that extraordinary rendition is immoral and hurts U.S. intelligence activities. Tim Naftali, in a 2005 article in *Slate*, discussed an incident in which the Bush administration kidnapped an alleged terrorist in Italy and rendered him to Egypt. Naftali says that this hurt the Bush administration's antiterrorism effort since destroying terrorist group al Qaeda required "consistently showing that we are the good guys—in other words, that we respect self-determination, democracy, and civil liberties." Sangitha Mc-Kenzie Millar agreed in a 2008 article on Antiwar.com in which she said that extraordinary rendition "is a powerful recruiting tool for al-Qaeda," and that it has "made cooperation between U.S. and European police and intelligence agencies more difficult." She added that rendition is a poor way of obtaining information since "intelligence gathered as a result of interrogations involving torture is not always accurate because it is obtained under extreme duress."

In the following viewpoints, commentators debate whether torture should play a role in U.S. intelligence efforts.

> *"The intelligence acquired from these interrogations has been a key reason why al Qaeda has failed to launch a spectacular attack in the West since 11 September 2001."*

Enhanced Interrogation Has Been Effective at Gathering Intelligence

Marc A. Thiessen

Marc A. Thiessen is a former speechwriter for President George W. Bush and the author of Courting Disaster: How the CIA Kept America Safe and How Barack Obama Is Inviting the Next Attack. *In the following viewpoint, Thiessen argues that enhanced interrogation techniques caused terrorists to provide authorities with useful information that saved lives. Thiessen states that the Barack Obama administration has endangered American lives by releasing details of the enhanced interrogation program, since terrorists will now be prepared to resist the American interrogation techniques.*

Marc A. Thiessen, "The CIA's Questioning Worked," *Washington Post*, April 21, 2009. Reproduced by permission of the author.

As you read, consider the following questions:

1. According to Thiessen, what intelligence did the CIA get from terrorist Khalid Sheik Mohammed before they started using enhanced techniques?

2. The author says the Obama administration redacted, or blacked out, information relating to what sort of information?

3. CIA director Leon Panetta said the Obama administration might use enhanced interrogation techniques under what circumstances, according to Thiessen?

In releasing highly classified documents on the CIA interrogation program last week [April 2009], President [Barack] Obama declared that the techniques used to question captured terrorists "did not make us safer."[1] This is patently false. The proof is in the memos Obama made public—in sections that have gone virtually unreported in the media.

Consider the Justice Department memo of May 30, 2005. It notes that "the CIA believes 'the intelligence acquired from these interrogations has been a key reason why al Qaeda [terrorist organization] has failed to launch a spectacular attack in the West since 11 September 2001.' ... In particular, the CIA believes that it would have been unable to obtain critical information from numerous detainees, including [Khalid Sheik Mohammed (KSM)] and Abu Zubaydah, without these enhanced techniques." The memo continues: "Before the CIA used enhanced techniques ... KSM resisted giving any answers to questions about future attacks, simply noting, 'Soon you will find out.'" Once the techniques were applied, "interrogations have led to specific, actionable intelligence, as well as a general increase in the amount of intelligence regarding al Qaeda and its affiliates."

1. The techniques in question are referred to as "enhanced interrogation" by supporters and as "torture" by those who oppose them.

Specifically, interrogation with enhanced techniques "led to the discovery of a KSM plot, the 'Second Wave,' 'to use East Asian operatives to crash a hijacked airliner into' a building in Los Angeles." KSM later acknowledged before a military commission at Guantanamo Bay [a U.S. military prison facility in Cuba] that the target was the Library Tower, the tallest building on the West Coast. The memo explains that "information obtained from KSM also led to the capture of Riduan bin Isomuddin, better known as Hambali, and the discovery of the Guraba Cell, a 17-member Jemmah Islamiyah [a militant Southeast Asian Islamic organization] cell tasked with executing the 'Second Wave.'" In other words, without enhanced interrogations, there could be a hole in the ground in Los Angeles to match the one in New York.

The memo notes that "[i]nterrogations of [Abu] Zubaydah—again, once enhanced techniques were employed—furnished detailed information regarding al Qaeda's 'organizational structure, key operatives, and modus operandi' and identified KSM as the mastermind of the September 11 attacks." This information helped the intelligence community plan the operation that captured KSM. It went on: "Zubaydah and KSM also supplied important information about [Abu Musab] al-Zarqawi and his network" in Iraq, which helped our operations against al-Qaeda in that country.

All this confirms information that I and others have described publicly. But just as the memo begins to describe previously undisclosed details of what enhanced interrogations achieved, the page is almost entirely blacked out. The Obama administration released pages of unredacted classified information on the techniques used to question captured terrorist leaders but pulled out its black marker when it came to the details of what those interrogations achieved.

KSM Talked After Enhanced Interrogation

Khalid Sheik Mohammed] KSM [transformed] from an avowed and truculent enemy of the United States into what the CIA called its "preeminent source" on al-Qaeda [the terrorist organization responsible for 9/11]. This reversal occurred after Mohammed was subjected to simulated drowning [waterboarding] and prolonged sleep deprivation, among other harsh interrogation techniques.

"KSM, an accomplished resistor, provided only a few intelligence reports prior to the use of the waterboard, ..." according to newly unclassified portions of a 2004 report by the CIA's then-inspector general.

Peter Finn, Joby Warrick, and Julie Tate,
Washington Post, August 29, 2009.

Obama Released Wrong Information

Yet there is more information confirming the program's effectiveness. The Office of Legal Counsel memo states "we discuss only a small fraction of the important intelligence CIA interrogators have obtained from KSM" and notes that "intelligence derived from CIA detainees has resulted in more than 6,000 intelligence reports and, in 2004, accounted for approximately half of the [Counterterrorism Center's] reporting on al Qaeda." The memos refer to other classified documents—including an "Effectiveness Memo" and an "IG [Inspector General] Report," which explain how "the use of enhanced techniques in the interrogations of KSM, Zubaydah and others ... has yielded critical information." Why didn't Obama officials release this information as well? Because they know that if the public could see the details of the techniques side by side with evidence that the program saved American lives, the vast majority would support continuing it.

Critics claim that enhanced techniques do not produce good intelligence because people will say anything to get the techniques to stop. But the memos note that, "as Abu Zubaydah himself explained with respect to enhanced techniques, 'brothers who are captured and interrogated are permitted by Allah to provide information when they believe they have reached the limit of their ability to withhold it in the face of psychological and physical hardship.'" In other words, the terrorists are called by their faith to resist as far as they can—and once they have done so, they are free to tell everything they know. This is because of their belief that "Islam will ultimately dominate the world and that this victory is inevitable." The job of the interrogator is to safely help the terrorist do his duty to Allah, so he then feels liberated to speak freely.

This is the secret to the program's success. And the Obama administration's decision to share this secret with the terrorists threatens our national security. Al-Qaeda will use this information and other details in the memos to train its operatives to resist questioning and withhold information on planned attacks. CIA Director Leon Panetta said during his confirmation hearings that even the Obama administration might use some of the enhanced techniques in a "ticking time bomb" scenario [that is, in a case where there is immediate danger to large numbers of people]. What will the administration do now that it has shared the limits of our interrogation techniques with the enemy? President Obama's decision to release these documents is one of the most dangerous and irresponsible acts ever by an American president during a time of war—and Americans may die as a result.

> *"Interrogation methods based on build-*
> *ing a relationship and on intellectual*
> *engagement were far more effective*
> *than intimidation and coercion."*

Torture Is Not an Effective Intelligence-Gathering Technique

Matthew Alexander

Matthew Alexander is a U.S. Air Force veteran and the author of How to Break a Terrorist: The U.S. Interrogators Who Used Brains, Not Brutality, to Take Down the Deadliest Man in Iraq. *He writes under a pseudonym for security reasons. In the following viewpoint, he discusses his experiences as an interrogator in Iraq. Alexander argues that most valuable intelligence does not come from torture but from conversation and points to his own successes in noncoercively gathering intelligence to track down terrorist leaders in Iraq. He concludes that torture undermines American intelligence efforts and should be banned.*

As you read, consider the following questions:

1. According to Alexander, how did Naji's parents die?

Matthew Alexander, "Talk, Not Torture, Gets the Information," *Los Angeles Times*, December 30, 2008. Reproduced by permission of the author.

2. Who does the author say Naji's father was, based on the information Naji provided?

3. How many interrogations does Alexander say he conducted and how many did he supervise?

He was only 12 years old, but he knew how to sling invective.

"You Americans are infidels, and you deserve to die." A skinny kid with a black head of hair and soft brown eyes, Naji had been brought to the Iraqi prison where I worked as an interrogator after his parents were killed. They died when the suicide bombers they'd been hosting blew themselves up to avoid being arrested. But Naji didn't yet know that he was an orphan, and he was furious at having been captured by the Americans.

Steve, one of a team of interrogators who worked for me, responded to the boy's tirade politely.

"Don't you think we're all just people and we need to get along?" Steve asked, speaking through our interpreter, Biggie. Naji, who's name I have changed to protect his identity, shook his head violently.

"No," Biggie translated. "You're all infidel pigs! I can't wait until I'm old enough to cut your heads off!"

There is more than one approach to extracting information from a captive. Interrogators are often encouraged to use threats and intimidation—and even harsher methods. But my small group of Air Force investigators, along with several military and civilian interrogators on my team, were committed to a different way. We believed that interrogation methods based on building a relationship and on intellectual engagement were far more effective than intimidation and coercion.

As I watched the interrogation from the monitoring room, Naji's invective seemed almost funny coming from such a scrawny kid. But it was a sign of how thoroughly he had embraced the Al Qaeda [the terrorist organization responsible for the September 11, 2001, attacks] propaganda he had heard at home. We had to hope he was not the face of Iraq's future.

"Do you know who this is?" Steve asked, showing Naji a photo of Abu Musab Zarqawi, the leader of Al Qaeda in Iraq.

"Of course, that is Abu Musab Zarqawi. He is our hero."

"Your hero?"

"Of course! When we play, the tallest, biggest kid gets to be Zarqawi."

In response to Steve's probing questions, Naji proudly explained that his father was grooming him to be a mujahedin [Islamic freedom fighter] and a future leader of Al Qaeda. He also said that his father took him to important meetings.

A veteran interrogator the night before had told us we "should show the little punk who's in charge." This was the attitude of many of the old guard, the interrogators who had been at Guantanamo Bay [a U.S. prison for terrorist suspects in Cuba] and in Afghanistan and Iraq early in the war, [the invasion of Afghanistan took place in 2001; of Iraq in 2003] when the "gloves were off." They mocked those of us who didn't imitate their methods of interrogation, which were based on fear and control. There was tremendous peer pressure to follow in their footsteps and not appear soft on our enemies.

Interviewing, Not Interrogating

We ignored the pressure. We believed that, particularly with a child, interviewing rather than interrogation got better results. Steve had been trained in interviewing children, and he used those skills with Naji, gently stroking the child's ego and noting that he must have been a very important boy to have attended meetings. Soon, Naji started rattling off places where meetings had taken place. He detailed who was at the gatherings, how many guns were stored at the houses, what was discussed and what plans were made. Naji talked because Steve was sympathetic and made him feel good.

A Recruitment Tool for Terrorists

The use of waterboarding and other torture techniques was a powerful recruitment tool for Al Qaeda [the terrorist organization responsible for the September 11, 2001, attacks]; it spawned thousands of would-be suicide bombers. [George W. Bush administration speechwriter and author Marc] Thiessen claims that we gained "intelligence" by using these torture techniques. But this shows that he knows nothing about the intelligence process or how our enemy grows and sustains itself.

Scott Horton, Harper's Magazine, *April 30, 2010.*

From the information he provided, it was clear that Naji's father had been a mid- to high-level Al Qaeda leader with connections throughout Yousifiya and Al Anbar province [in Iraq]. By the time the interview ended after an hour, Steve had filled up pages in his notebook with detailed information about Naji's father's network.

Back in our office, Steve and I marveled at all the intelligence Naji had provided—the names, the locations. He'd pinpointed the better part of Al Qaeda's operations around Yousifiya. In the two weeks that followed, our soldiers put this information to good use and took out a significant portion of Al Qaeda's suicide-bombing network in the area. For two weeks, violence dropped and many lives were saved.

During my time in Iraq, I personally conducted 300 interrogations and supervised more than 1,000. Naji was the most committed Al Qaeda member I met during that time. He and his father, who had clearly joined the group because they bought into the ideology, represented a very small percentage of the Sunni Iraqis [the largest branch of Islam, to which al

Qaeda and many Iraqis belong]. The overwhelming majority of Sunni Iraqis I interviewed joined for other reasons—economic need, to meet tribal obligations or, most common of all, to get protection from Shiite [a branch of Islam to which the majority of Iraqis belong] militias.

Good Interrogation Uses Negotiation

I interviewed Naji twice during the week after his first interview. By the end of his stay with us, after we had coddled him, ensured his comfort and treated him with affection despite his contempt for us, he started to warm up. By the day before he left, his vituperative speech had disappeared completely.

Good interrogation is not an exercise in domination or control. It's an opportunity for negotiation and compromise. It's a common ground where the two sides in this war meet, and it's a grand stage where words become giants, tears flow like rivers and emotions rage like wildfires. It is a forum in which we should always display America's strengths—cultural understanding, tolerance, compassion and intellect. But that's not how all interrogators see their role.

According to a recent report from the bipartisan Senate Armed Services Committee, "The abuse of detainees in U.S. custody cannot be attributed to the actions of a 'few bad apples' acting on their own." The effects of the policy that allowed torture to happen at Guantanamo Bay, the report concluded, spread to Iraq through the interrogators who had first been at Guantanamo. The preference for harsh interrogation techniques was extremely counterproductive and harmed our ability to obtain cooperation from Al Qaeda detainees. Even after the old guard interrogators were forced to play by the rules of the Geneva Convention, [an international agreement governing treatment of prisoners of war,] there was still plenty of leeway for interrogation methods based on fear and control. I believe their continued reliance on such techniques has severely hampered our ability to stop terrorist attacks against U.S. forces and Iraqi civilians.

We will win this war by being smarter, not harsher. For those who would accuse me of being too nice to our enemies, I encourage you to examine our success in hunting down Zarqawi and his network. The drop in suicide bombings in Iraq at two points in the spring and summer of 2006 was a direct result of our smarter interrogation methods.

I used to tell my team in Iraq: "The things that make you a good American are the things that will make you a good interrogator." We must outlaw torture across every agency of our government, restore our adherence to the American principles passed down to us and, in doing so, better protect Americans from future terrorist attacks.

> "The International Convention Against Torture, adopted by the United States in 1994, compels the US to prosecute everyone who is responsible for torture."

CIA Agents Used Torture and Should Be Prosecuted

Larry Cox

Larry Cox is the executive director of the humanitarian group Amnesty International USA. In the following viewpoint, he argues that international law requires the prosecution of all those in the George W. Bush administration who participated in or abetted torture. This includes Central Intelligence Agency (CIA) agents who conducted torture and government officials who authorized it. Cox says that quick prosecutions are necessary to avoid the statute of limitations on some offenses. He concludes that failure to act will damage America's global standing and will encourage terrorist recruiting.

Larry Cox, "Obama Must Prosecute Bush-Era Torture Enablers," *Christian Science Monitor*, June 15, 2009. Copyright © The Christian Science Monitor. Reproduced by permission of the author.

As you read, consider the following questions:

1. According to the author, what is the statute of limitations on torture crimes committed in the months leading up to September 2002?
2. Why does Cox believe that the Senate Intelligence Committee report will not break much new ground?
3. The author says that the 2005 Detainee Treatment Act provides legal cover to torturers by including what defense?

With [former vice president] Dick Cheney and the infamous torture memos making headlines,[1] President [Barack] Obama and our nation face a choice. Should they prosecute or protect those responsible for the torture of detainees in secret CIA detention centers? If our leaders wish to steer our country back to the right side of the law, they must act immediately and unequivocally to prosecute.

The problem is that leading senators want the Senate Select Committee on Intelligence to complete its investigation into the treatment and interrogation of detainees (which could take between four and six months), before any prosecution is launched. Yet such a delay would potentially risk running out the clock on certain types of prosecution.

The federal Anti-Torture Act, for example, is subject to a statute of limitations after only eight years. For the prosecution of crimes committed in the months leading up to September 2002—when [George W.] Bush administration lawyers produced the first of the "torture memos" that purported to make torture legally permissible—that expiration date is spring 2010.

But there is no need to wait that long. There is already ample evidence that shows the previous administration

1. In April 2009, the Barack Obama administration released memos issued by the George W. Bush Justice Department. The memos argued that extreme interrogation techniques were not torture and were legal. The memos were used to justify practices that many critics consider to be torture.

concocted, approved, and implemented a torture policy. What's more, there is no legal imperative holding the Department of Justice or federal prosecutors back from launching a criminal investigation, beginning with the task of identifying who is responsible for the crimes that have already been documented.

Although the Senate Intelligence Committee report may eventually provide some insights, it cannot be a substitute for the criminal investigations required for prosecution. But given the committee's possible complicity in allowing torture to continue despite multiple Central Intelligence Agency briefings, we should not expect its report to break much new ground.

When Mr. Obama rescinded the torture memos upon taking office, he took an important first step toward repairing the damage wrought by the previous administration on our country's commitment to human rights and rule of law. But his statement in April [2009] to forgo prosecution of those CIA agents who carried out torture is a breach of international law.

Some critics argue that a full investigation might lead the US public to ultimately side with torture and thus prosecution could be politically counterproductive. Others argue that prosecuting hundreds of people would waste resources during a war on terror, and that it should stay focused on going after terrorists.

International Law Demands Prosecution

However, the International Convention Against Torture, adopted by the United States in 1994, compels the US to prosecute everyone who is responsible for torture, all the way up the chain of command to top government officials who authorize it. Obama himself said in April that he's "a strong believer that it's important to look forward and not backwards, and to remind ourselves that we do have very real security threats out there." At the same time he also said that "nobody

Prosecutions May Be Opened

The Justice Department's ethics office has recommended reversing the [George W.] Bush administration and reopening nearly a dozen prisoner-abuse cases, potentially exposing [Central Intelligence Agency (CIA)] employees and contractors to prosecution for brutal treatment of terrorism suspects. . . .

It now [in August 2009] seems all but certain that the appointment of a prosecutor or other concrete steps will follow.

David Johnston, New York Times, August 24, 2009.

is above the law, and if there are clear instances of wrongdoing, that people should be prosecuted just like any ordinary citizen." The law allows no exceptions.

Congress also has an urgent and important role to play: It must eliminate a loophole written into the 2005 Detainee Treatment Act. That piece of legislation contains provisions that were crafted to provide legal cover to torturers. This includes the defense that those who committed torture believed the acts were legal at the time, since they had been interpreted as such by the White House torture memos (none of which carried the force of law).

Legislators must also attend to the back end of the accountability process by eliminating or extending the statute of limitations beyond 2010, as Rep. John Conyers (D) of Michigan has proposed.

Efforts to hold torturers and torture enablers accountable have been launched abroad, most notably in Germany, Italy, and Spain.

Spanish magistrate Baltasar Garzón, a central figure in the prosecution of [Chilean dictator] General Augusto Pinochet, is an example of a quick, effective actor. He recently launched an investigation into the Bush administration last month [May 2009] over the alleged torture of four Spanish nationals at Guantánamo [Bay, a U.S. prison facility for terrorists in Cuba] under the legal principle of universal jurisdiction.

He also has ordered an inquiry into whether or not six former Bush administration lawyers created a legal framework to permit torture.

Should the Spanish court ultimately indict anyone pursuant to these claims, it is unclear whether the Obama administration would extradite former US officials. But such a development might, at the very least, prevent those former officials from traveling anywhere in the European Union and further discredit their already tainted legacies.

The Obama administration promised a new era of international cooperation and respect. It now faces the first major test of its rhetoric. If the US fails to prosecute those responsible for torture, we can take our place alongside countries we have long criticized for privileging politics over justice and accountability by letting criminals go free.

Beyond the United States' global standing, the former administration's policies also made Americans less safe by providing recruiting tools for terrorists. The Obama administration must show that such abuses won't stand.

> "Even the worst of the CIA techniques
> that were authorized—waterboard-
> ing—would not constitute torture."

CIA Agents Did Not Use Torture

Jeffrey Addicott

Jeffrey Addicott is a professor at St. Mary's University School of Law and a former lieutenant colonel in the U.S. Army Judge Advocate General's Corps. In the following viewpoint, he argues that not all mistreatment of prisoners is torture, and that only torture should be prosecuted. He says that according to international standards, the interrogation techniques authorized by the George W. Bush Justice Department did not rise to the level of torture. Therefore, he says, Central Intelligence Agency (CIA) agents who used the Bush-authorized interrogation techniques should not be prosecuted.

As you read, consider the following questions:

1. What does Addicott say must be done if the Bush Department of Justice memos authorized techniques that constitute torture?

2. What common law doctrine does the author say the accused on trial for torture would be able to argue?

Jeffrey Addicott, "No Torture, No Prosecution," *Jurist*, May 8, 2009. Reproduced by permission.

3. What does Addicott say is the leading international case in the realm of defining "severe pain and suffering"?

Allegations of torture roll off the tongue with ease. In the context of American interrogation practices and treatment of both terrorist detainees and enemy combatant detainees, false allegations of "torture" have been regularly raised by a wide variety of individuals and interest groups, the latest round of concern being the recently [as of May 2009] released [George W.] Bush Department of Justice "CIA" memorandums. In short, if the memos authorized techniques which constitute torture, then the rule of law is absolute—those who approved, those who authorized, and those who committed the acts must be prosecuted in a court of law. On the other hand, if the interrogation practices authorized did not constitute torture, then there is no need to prosecute (or to engage in the endless political grandstanding).

Mistreatment Not Always Torture

Recognizing that not every alleged incident of mistreatment necessarily satisfies the legal definition of torture, it is imperative that one view such allegations with a clear understanding of the applicable legal standards set out in law and judicial precedent. In this manner, claims of illegal interrogation practices can be properly measured as falling above or below a particular legal threshold. Only then can one hope to set aside the worn-out rhetoric by such groups as [the humanitarian organization] Amnesty International, who call the Guantanamo [Bay, Cuba,] detention facility [housing U.S. terrorism suspects] the "gulag [a Soviet prison camp] of our time."

The 1984 United Nations Convention Against Torture, and Other Cruel, Inhuman or Degrading Treatment or Punishment (Torture Convention) is the primary international agreement governing torture and lesser forms of coercion known as "ill-treatment." All nations must abide by the provisions and prosecute anyone who ordered or carried out torture. Article 2 of the Torture Convention absolutely excludes the notion of exceptional circumstances to serve as an excuse to the prohibition of torture. "No exceptional circumstances whatsoever, whether a state of war or a threat of war, internal political instability or any other public emergency, may be invoked as a justification for torture."

Nevertheless, the accused on trial for torture is certainly able to argue the common law [law developed by court precedent] doctrine of "necessity" at his trial—the defendant committed an evil (torture) to prevent a greater evil (mass murder). If the jury accepts this defense, the defendant will be found not guilty.

Criteria for Torture

According to the Torture Convention, for torture to exist the following criteria must be present: (1) the act must be intentional; (2) it must be performed by a State agent; (3) the act must cause severe pain or suffering to body or mind; and (4) it must be accomplished with the intent to gain information or a confession.

In the Anglo-Saxon legal tradition, we generally look to authoritative judicial decisions to define key terms in treaty and legislation. Perhaps the leading international case in the realm of defining "severe pain or suffering" in the context of interrogation practices comes from the often cited European Court of Human Rights ruling, *Ireland v. United Kingdom*. By an overwhelming majority vote, the *Ireland* court found certain interrogation practices of British authorities to interrogate suspected terrorism in Northern Ireland to be "inhuman and degrading," i.e., ill-treatment, but not severe enough to rise to the level of torture. According to the Court, the finding of ill-treatment rather than torture "derives principally from a difference in the intensity of the suffering inflicted." In *Ireland*, the Court considered the use of five investigative measures known as "the five techniques" which were practiced by British authorities for periods of "four or five" days pending or during interrogation sessions.

- Wall-standing: Forcing the detainee to stand for some period of hours in a stress position described as "spread-eagled against the wall, with their fingers put high above their head against the wall, the legs spread apart and the feet back, causing them to stand on their toes with the weight of the body mainly on the fingers." Wall-standing was practiced for up to 30 hours with occasional periods for rest.

- Hooding: Placing a dark hood over the head of the detainee and keeping it on for prolonged periods of time.

- Subjection to noise: Holding the detainee in a room where there was a continuous loud and hissing noise.

- Deprivation of Sleep: Depriving detainee of sleep for prolonged periods of time.

- Deprivation of Food and Drink: Reducing the food and drink to suspects pending interrogations.

Considering the level of interrogation standards set out in the *Ireland* case, the conclusion is clear. Even the worst of the CIA techniques that were authorized—waterboarding [a technique in which victims are subjected to controlled drowning]—would not constitute torture (the CIA method is similar to what we have done hundreds and hundreds of times to our own military special operations soldiers in military training courses on escape and survival).

> "It would make very 'bad law,' and would create a legal precedent that would haunt our criminal justice system for generations, if we cede to the demands of those calling for torture prosecutions."

CIA Agents Who Used Torture Should Not Be Prosecuted

Harvey Silverglate

Harvey Silverglate is a criminal defense and civil liberties lawyer. In the following viewpoint, he argues that even if Central Intelligence Agency (CIA) agents did torture prisoners, they did so only because they had been told by authorities that their actions were legal. Since they did not know they were acting illegally, and since juries probably would not convict them in any case, Silverglate concludes that prosecuting the agents would only further damage civil liberties.

As you read, consider the following questions:

1. What does the American Civil Liberties Union of Massachusetts argue we would be accepting if we do not

Harvey Silverglate, "On Torture Outrage, Let's Take a Step Back," *The Boston Globe*, April 23, 2009. Copyright © 2009 Globe Newspaper Company. Reproduced by permission of the author.

prosecute CIA agents who used torture, according to Silverglate?

2. Why does the author say that the Department of Justice torture memos are different from anything in the Nazi and Soviet eras?

3. What steps does Silverglate say are being taken short of prosecution?

"Hard cases make bad law." So goes the hoary aphorism taught to generations of law students and invoked by lawyers and judges tempted to do what the heart implores but the rational mind warns—or should warn—against. The debate on whether to prosecute intelligence agents who inflicted what civilized citizens reasonably deem "torture," but what Department of Justice [DOJ] legal memoranda advised was nonetheless lawful, exemplifies the occasional "hard case."

Prosecutions Would Damage Civil Liberties

But it would make very "bad law," and would create a legal precedent that would haunt our criminal justice system for generations, if we cede to the demands of those calling for torture prosecutions. The primary objection to such prosecutions is that they would deal a body blow to civil liberties.

The American Civil Liberties Union of Massachusetts, where I am a board member, argues that if we do not prosecute the agents, we would be implicitly accepting "the so-called superior orders defense" [the idea that a person ordered to do something by a superior is not responsible for that action] correctly rejected by the Nuremberg war crimes tribunal [that tried Nazi war criminals]. Indeed, the "torture memos" have a touch of the style of history's more infamous Nazi operatives, where evil niceties of human abuse were discussed with a chilling precision that only bureaucratese could supply. Still, however disturbing the DOJ torture memos are, they are far from anything seen in the Nazi and Soviet eras. They approve the infliction of terror and pain, but not disfigurement and death.

What is the importance of this distinction? A CIA agent, operating in good faith, could readily consider such DOJ advice to be a binding legal opinion that he could safely follow. And in our legal system, based on an ancient Anglo-Saxon moral and legal tenet incorporated into our own criminal codes, a wrongdoer may be punished only if he knowingly and intentionally committed an act that he believed to be illegal. Given the facts and circumstances—the nation had just withstood the worst terrorist attack in its history and was being led by a president who suddenly declared a full-scale "war on terror"—it is inconceivable that any criminal jury in any American jurisdiction could, would, or even should agree unanimously (which is what it takes to convict) that an agent, acting in accord with DOJ legal advice, is guilty beyond a reasonable doubt (another prerequisite for conviction). These are legal realities often missed by those outside the practice of trial law.

Use Penalties Short of Prosecution

Unless we are prepared to allow the war on terror to inflict further damage on our legal system, we need to step back and ask if perhaps better sense, and cooler heads, should prevail in the face of righteous outrage at our government's conduct. Steps might be taken short of prosecution. Ethics investigations could be (and indeed are being) conducted of the Department of Justice lawyers who drafted the memos—among them current [University of California at] Berkeley law professor John Yoo and sitting federal appellate judge Jay Bybee. Discipline could include disbarment as well as judicial impeachment. But prosecutions could, and likely would, wreak havoc on principles that civil libertarians should seek to protect, not evade.

Releasing Torture Memos Will Undermine Intelligence Morale

The end effect of the . . . release [in April 2009 of Justice Department memos justifying torture] is that people who have put their lives on the line in U.S. counterterrorism efforts are now uncertain of whether they should be making that sacrifice. . . .

The memos' release will not have a catastrophic effect on U.S. counterterrorism efforts. Indeed, most of the information in the memos was leaked to the press years ago. However, when the release . . . is examined in a wider context, and combined with a few other dynamics, it appears that the U.S. counterterrorism community is quietly slipping back into an atmosphere of risk-aversion and malaise—an atmosphere not dissimilar to that described by the . . . [9/11 Commission] as a contributing factor to the intelligence failures that led to the 9/11 attacks.

Fred Burton and Scott Stewart, STRATFOR,
April 29, 2009. www.stratfor.com.

In his memorable play "A Man for All Seasons," Robert Bolt depicts a fictional but profoundly truthful discussion between Sir Thomas More, the cleric who followed his conscience during the tyrannical reign of King Henry VIII, and William Roper, who undertakes to warn More to take preemptive action against the ambitious Richard Rich. "Arrest him," Roper advises. "For what?" queries More, ever the student of law. "That man's bad," chimes in a courtier. "There is no law against being bad," counters More. Roper protests that if the laws of England are analogous to trees in a forest, and if the devil were hiding behind a tree, "I'd cut down every law in

England" to get him. More responds with one of western literature's most profound explanations of the rule of law in safeguarding liberty. "Oh? And when the last law was down, and the Devil turned round on you—where would you hide, Roper, the laws all being flat?"

More's conclusion rings true today: "Yes, I give the Devil benefit of law, for my own safety's sake!"

| "The use of torture was not part of a competent intelligence effort, but a response to a massive intelligence failure."

Torture Was a Desperate Response to Intelligence Failure

George Friedman

George Friedman is the founder and CEO of the private intelligence corporation STRATFOR. In the following viewpoint, he argues that there was a decade-long failure of intelligence following the fall of the Soviet Union in 1989. As a result, Friedman says, the George W. Bush administration after September 11, 2001, knew little about al Qaeda, the terrorist organization responsible for the attack. The lack of knowledge led to the use of torture in a desperate effort to gain more information. Friedman maintains that resorting to torture was understandable given the intelligence failures, but that it continued after the emergency had passed.

As you read, consider the following questions:

1. Friedman says that it was reasonable to assume that al Qaeda cells were operating where following 9/11?

George Friedman, "Torture and the U.S. Intelligence Failure," STRATFOR, April 20, 2009. Reproduced by permission.

2. What does the author say that the president's oath to protect the Constitution means in practical terms?

3. What does Friedman say is the problem with torture in the hands of bureaucracies?

The [Barack] Obama administration published [in April 2009] a series of memoranda on torture issued under the [George W.] Bush administration. The memoranda, most of which dated from the period after 9/11, [2001,] authorized measures including depriving prisoners of solid food, having them stand shackled and in uncomfortable positions, leaving them in cold cells with inadequate clothing, slapping their heads and/or abdomens, and telling them that their families might be harmed if they didn't cooperate with their interrogators.

On the scale of human cruelty, these actions do not rise anywhere near the top. At the same time, anyone who thinks that being placed without food in a freezing cell subject to random mild beatings—all while being told that your family might be joining you—isn't agonizing clearly lacks imagination. The treatment of detainees could have been worse. It was terrible nonetheless.

Torture and the Intelligence Gap

But torture is meant to be terrible, and we must judge the torturer in the context of his own desperation. In the wake of 9/11, anyone who wasn't terrified was not in touch with reality. We know several people who now are quite blasé about 9/11. Unfortunately for them, we knew them in the months after, and they were not nearly as composed then as they are now.

Sept. 11 was terrifying for one main reason: We had little idea about al Qaeda's capabilities. It was a very reasonable assumption that other al Qaeda cells were operating in the

United States and that any day might bring follow-on attacks. (Especially given the group's reputation for one-two attacks.) We still remember our first flight after 9/11, looking at our fellow passengers, planning what we would do if one of them moved. Every time a passenger visited the lavatory, one could see the tensions soar.

And while Sept. 11 was frightening enough, there were ample fears that al Qaeda had secured a "suitcase bomb" [that is, a nuclear weapon small enough to fit in a suitcase] and that a nuclear attack on a major U.S. city could come at any moment. For individuals, such an attack was simply another possibility. We remember staying at a hotel in Washington close to the White House and realizing that we were at ground zero—and imagining what the next moment might be like. For the government, however, the problem was having scraps of intelligence indicating that al Qaeda might have a nuclear weapon, but not having any way of telling whether those scraps had any value. The president and vice president accordingly were continually kept at different locations, and not for any frivolous reason.

This lack of intelligence led directly to the most extreme fears, which in turn led to extreme measures. Washington simply did not know very much about al Qaeda and its capabilities and intentions in the United States. A lack of knowledge forces people to think of worst-case scenarios. In the absence of intelligence to the contrary after 9/11, the only reasonable assumption was that al Qaeda was planning more—and perhaps worse—attacks.

Collecting intelligence rapidly became the highest national priority. Given the genuine and reasonable fears, no action in pursuit of intelligence was out of the question, so long as it promised quick answers. This led to the authorization of torture, among other things. Torture offered a rapid means to accumulate intelligence, or at least—given the time lag on other means—it was something that had to be tried.

Torture and the Moral Question

And this raises the moral question. The United States is a moral project: its Declaration of Independence and Constitution state that. The president takes an oath to preserve, protect and defend the Constitution from all enemies foreign and domestic. The Constitution does not speak to the question of torture of non-citizens, but it implies an abhorrence of rights violations (at least for citizens). But the Declaration of Independence contains the phrase, "a decent respect for the opinions of mankind." This indicates that world opinion matters.

At the same time, the president is sworn to protect the Constitution. In practical terms, this means protecting the physical security of the United States "against all enemies, foreign and domestic." Protecting the principles of the declaration and the Constitution are meaningless without regime preservation and defending the nation.

While this all makes for an interesting seminar in political philosophy, presidents—and others who have taken the same oath—do not have the luxury of the contemplative life. They must act on their oaths, and inaction is an action. Former U.S. President George W. Bush knew that he did not know the threat, and that in order to carry out his oath, he needed very rapidly to find out the threat. He could not know that torture would work, but he clearly did not feel that he had the right to avoid it.

Consider this example. Assume you knew that a certain individual knew the location of a nuclear device planted in an American city. The device would kill hundreds of thousands of Americans, but the individual refused to divulge the information. Would anyone who had sworn the oath have the right not to torture the individual? Torture might or might not work, but either way, would it be moral to protect the individual's rights while allowing hundreds of thousands to die? It would seem that in this case, torture is a moral imperative; the rights of the one with the information cannot transcend the life of a city.

Torture in the Real World

But here is the problem: You would not find yourself in this situation. Knowing a bomb had been planted, knowing who knew that the bomb had been planted, and needing only to apply torture to extract this information is not how the real world works. Post-9/11, the United States knew much less about the extent of the threat from al Qaeda. This hypothetical sort of torture was not the issue.

Discrete information was not needed, but situational awareness. The United States did not know what it needed to know, it did not know who was of value and who wasn't, and it did not know how much time it had. Torture thus was not a precise solution to a specific problem: It became an intelligence-gathering technique. The nature of the problem the United States faced forced it into indiscriminate intelligence gathering. When you don't know what you need to know, you cast a wide net. And when torture is included in the mix, it is cast wide as well. In such a case, you know you will be following many false leads—and when you carry torture with you, you will be torturing people with little to tell you. Moreover, torture applied by anyone other than well-trained, experienced personnel (who are in exceptionally short supply) will only compound these problems, and make the practice less productive.

Defenders of torture frequently seem to believe that the person in custody is known to have valuable information, and that this information must be forced out of him. His possession of the information is proof of his guilt. The problem is that unless you have excellent intelligence to begin with, you will become engaged in developing baseline intelligence, and the person you are torturing may well know nothing at all. Torture thus becomes not only a waste of time and a violation of decency, it actually undermines good intelligence. After a while, scooping up suspects in a dragnet and trying to extract intelligence becomes a substitute for competent intelligence techniques—and can potentially blind the intelligence service. This is especially true as people will tell you what they think you want to hear to make torture stop.

Critics of torture, on the other hand, seem to assume the torture was brutality for the sake of brutality instead of a desperate attempt to get some clarity on what might well have been a catastrophic outcome. The critics also cannot know the extent to which the use of torture actually prevented follow-on attacks. They assume that to the extent that torture was useful, it was not essential; that there were other ways to find out what was needed. In the long run, they might have been correct. But neither they, nor anyone else, had the right to assume in late 2001 that there was a long run. One of the things that wasn't known was how much time there was.

The U.S. Intelligence Failure

The endless argument over torture, the posturing of both critics and defenders, misses the crucial point. The United States turned to torture because it has experienced a massive intelligence failure reaching back a decade. The U.S. intelligence community simply failed to gather sufficient information on al Qaeda's intentions, capability, organization and personnel. The use of torture was not part of a competent intelligence effort, but a response to a massive intelligence failure.

That failure was rooted in a range of miscalculations over time. There was the public belief that the end of the Cold War meant the United States didn't need a major intelligence effort, a point made by the late Senator Daniel Moynihan. There were the intelligence people who regarded Afghanistan [which sheltered al Qaeda members] as old news. There was the Torricelli amendment [in the mid-1990s] that made recruiting people with ties to terrorist groups illegal without special approval. There were the Middle East experts who could not understand that al Qaeda was fundamentally different from anything seen before. The list of the guilty is endless, and ultimately includes the American people, who always seem to believe that the view of the world as a dangerous place is something made up by contractors and bureaucrats.

Bush was handed an impossible situation on Sept. 11, after just nine months in office. The country demanded protection, and given the intelligence shambles he inherited, he reacted about as well or badly as anyone else might have in the situation. He used the tools he had, and hoped they were good enough.

The problem with torture—as with other exceptional measures—is that it is useful, at best, in extraordinary situations. The problem with all such techniques in the hands of bureaucracies is that the extraordinary in due course becomes the routine, and torture as a desperate stopgap measure becomes a routine part of the intelligence interrogator's tool kit.

At a certain point, the emergency was over. U.S. intelligence had focused itself and had developed an increasingly coherent picture of al Qaeda, with the aid of allied Muslim intelligence agencies, and was able to start taking a toll on al Qaeda. The war had become routinized, and extraordinary measures were no longer essential. But the routinization of the extraordinary is the built-in danger of bureaucracy, and what began as a response to unprecedented dangers became part of the process. Bush had an opportunity to move beyond the emergency. He didn't.

If you know that an individual is loaded with information, torture can be a useful tool. But if you have so much intelligence that you already know enough to identify the individual is loaded with information, then you have come pretty close to winning the intelligence war. That's not when you use torture. That's when you simply point out to the prisoner that, "for you the war is over." You lay out all you already know and how much you know about him. That is as demoralizing as freezing in a cell—and helps your interrogators keep their balance.

U.S. President Barack Obama has handled this issue in the style to which we have become accustomed, and which is as practical a solution as possible. He has published the memos authorizing torture to make this entirely a Bush administration problem while refusing to prosecute anyone associated with torture, keeping the issue from becoming overly divisive. Good politics perhaps, but not something that deals with the fundamental question.

The fundamental question remains unanswered, and may remain unanswered. When a president takes an oath to "preserve, protect and defend the Constitution of the United States," what are the limits on his obligation? We take the oath for granted. But it should be considered carefully by anyone entering this debate, particularly for presidents.

> *"Torture is fundamentally at odds with the image of the United States as a country that will play by the rules, and that is how the FBI must be perceived in order to do its job."*

Torture Undermines the Effectiveness of the FBI

Asha Rangappa

Asha Rangappa is an associate dean at Yale Law School and a former special agent at the Federal Bureau of Investigation (FBI). In the following viewpoint, she argues that the FBI is often responsible for gathering foreign intelligence from foreign agents and from nationals in the United States. Rangappa says that goodwill toward the United States can often help FBI agents convince targets to share information. Rangappa concludes that the use of torture undermines such goodwill and will hurt the FBI's ability to gather intelligence.

As you read, consider the following questions:

1. What advantage does the FBI have over the Central Intelligence Agency in terms of obtaining intelligence, according to Rangappa?

2. How does the author say that FBI agent George Piro got Iraqi leader Saddam Hussein to talk?

3. What does Rangappa say are the most promising means of getting intelligence domestically?

Last week [September 2, 2009], President [Barack] Obama placed the FBI in charge of interrogating terrorism suspects abroad, removing the CIA from this role. Critics of this decision claim that we will get less intelligence as a result. But the CIA's use of torture has endangered our ability to get intelligence all along, right here at home.

The FBI Gathers Foreign Intelligence

The debate about the use of torture has focused on the CIA because it is the organization primarily responsible for gathering intelligence abroad. But a significant portion of our foreign intelligence is obtained within our own borders, by the FBI. That's because almost every country has its own foreign intelligence service—its version of the CIA—that sends agents to the United States to steal our defense secrets, commit economic espionage, and harass dissidents who have sought refuge here. The FBI has exclusive jurisdiction, as part of its counterintelligence mandate, to find out who these people are and what they are doing.

A second and arguably more important goal of the FBI is to persuade some of these people, or "targets," to change sides and share the information they have about their own governments and countries with us. It's the real-life James Bond scenario: developing "double agents" and obtaining critical foreign intelligence in the interest of national security. The FBI uses the fact that it operates on American soil to its advantage. FBI agents, unlike their CIA counterparts, can operate openly, rather than covertly. FBI agents also do not have to worry about hostile host governments discovering their activities and disrupting their intelligence networks. This means that the FBI is in a relatively strong position to produce a steady stream of valuable intelligence that is difficult to obtain abroad.

Some of these targets run afoul of the law during their stays in the United States. In those instances, threats, like that of deportation, can induce them to share the information they have. But most of these targets are not criminals. They are diplomats, scientists, or scholars with access to classified information or foreign nationals with important ties to their home countries. Consequently, the information they have to offer is obtained because they choose to give it. FBI agents must figure out what makes these people tick and in particular what will entice them to cooperate. This can include financial gain, educational opportunities for their children, medical treatment for themselves or a family member, or even the chance to stay in the United States and have a better life.

Goodwill Is an Intelligence Tool

But getting people to flip is primarily a psychological game rather than a material one. After all, the FBI is asking its targets to commit the ultimate act of disloyalty to their country—treason. Few people are willing to make this leap quickly, even in exchange for the most lucrative or attractive offer. It's an FBI agent's job to slowly win the target's trust and help him rationalize his decision to switch his allegiance. In my experience as a former FBI agent who both participated in and observed successful recruitments, it's much easier to do this when a target has, at some level, a sense of admiration and respect for the United States. A nugget of goodwill toward America offers an agent the chance to step in, gain the target's confidence, and convince him that playing for Team USA is worth the risk.

Policies like the use of torture make it more difficult for the FBI to develop relationships based on trust. Even when torture is used on a few people and in another country, and

The FBI and CIA Split on Torture

After [al Qaeda leader Osama Bin Laden's henchman] Mr. Zubaydah's capture, a C.I.A. interrogation team was dispatched from the agency's counterterrorism center to take the lead in his questioning, ... and F.B.I. agents were withdrawn. . . .

The new C.I.A. team concluded that ... more aggressive techniques were warranted.

F.B.I. agents on the scene angrily protested the more aggressive approach, arguing that persuasion rather than coercion had succeeded. But leaders of the C.I.A. interrogation team were convinced that tougher tactics were warranted and said that the methods had been authorized by senior lawyers at the White House.

David Johnston, New York Times, *September 10, 2006.*

by a different agency, it casts doubts on the U.S. government's overall willingness to act in good faith. Targets often project the skepticism about the United States that torture fosters onto individual FBI agents, who are often the only face of the government they see. In short, torture is fundamentally at odds with the image of the United States as a country that will play by the rules, and that is how the FBI must be perceived in order to do its job.

The FBI Has Been Effective

Whether President Obama's decision to put the FBI in charge of interrogating suspects abroad as well as at home will yield more or less information from terror suspects remains to be seen. The FBI's past success with some high-level detainees is promising: FBI agent George Piro, who was in charge of interrogating [Iraqi dictator] Saddam Hussein, was able to get the former dictator to talk by, among other things, reading his poetry, helping him plant a flower garden, and bringing him cookies on his birthday. More recently, former FBI agent Ali Soufan testified to Congress that he was able to gain information about [9/11 mastermind] Khalid Sheikh Mohammed from terrorist detainee Abu Zubaydah while nursing him back to health (and before the CIA began its harsher tactics, which Soufan argues backfired). Clearly, the FBI's traditional methods can work.

But whatever we conclude about the effectiveness of torture on terrorism suspects abroad, we will never use it to elicit information from people within the United States. That leaves trust and cooperation as our most promising means of getting intelligence domestically, and maintaining our good-guy image is vital to that effort. Any intelligence obtained through torture has to be balanced against the diminished capacity of the FBI to effectively exploit its intelligence base here at home. We should remember that when we calculate what kind of interrogation is a net gain or loss for national security.

Periodical Bibliography

The following articles have been selected to supplement the diverse views presented in this chapter.

Robert Alt and David Kaye   "A Chilling Effect on CIA Agents?" *Los Angeles Times*, August 26, 2009.

Anne Applebaum   "The Torture Myth," *Washington Post*, January 12, 2005.

Marcus Baram   "Opposition Grows to Obama's Decision Not to Prosecute CIA Agents," *Huffington Post*, April 19, 2009. www.huffingtonpost.com.

CBS News   "FBI: We Warned About Torture of Detainees," April 24, 2008. www.cbsnews.com.

Joseph Farah   "Waterboarding Is Not Torture," *WorldNet Daily*, January 2, 2008.

Jeremy R. Hammond   "Obama, American Ideals, and Torture as 'a Useful Tool,'" *Foreign Policy Journal*, April 21, 2009.

Katherine Harmon   "Did CIA Doctors Perform Torture Research on Detainees?" *Scientific American*, June 7, 2010.

Scott Horton   "Defending Enhanced Interrogation Techniques," *Harper's Magazine*, June 15, 2007.

Scott Horton   "'I Challenge Marc Thiessen'—Six Questions for Malcolm Nance," *Harper's Magazine*, April 30, 2010.

Andrew C. McCarthy   "Waterboarding and Torture," *National Review*, October 26, 2007.

Malcolm Nance   "Waterboarding Is Torture," *Small Wars Journal*, October 31, 2007.

Andy Sullivan   "Waterboarding Effective but Torture: Former CIA Agent," *International Business Times*, December 12, 2007.

Mark Tran   "FBI Files Detailed Guantanamo Torture Tactics," *Guardian* (Manchester, UK), January 3, 2007. www.guardian.co.uk.

For Further Discussion

Chapter 1

1. Both Gene Healy and Josh Filler suggest that politics have interfered with the mission of the Department of Homeland Security. What different political problems do they see, and how would they go about solving them?

2. On what grounds does Melvin A. Goodman argue that the 9/11 attacks were worse than Pearl Harbor? Is his argument convincing? Why or why not?

Chapter 2

1. In advocating for warrantless wiretapping, does Mortimer B. Zuckerman use any of the talking points attributed to wiretapping proponents by The Left Coaster Blog? If so, which ones does he use and what is The Left Coaster Blog's response to these talking points? Who of the two authors do you find more convincing? Why?

Chapter 3

1. Adam Entous and Sue Pleming describe an intelligence success in Afghanistan. Would this kind of success make Michael T. Flynn, Matt Pottinger, and Paul D. Batchelor change their minds about the failure of intelligence in Afghanistan? Why or why not?

2. John Judis argues that "the CIA was established to prevent unanticipated disasters." Would Roger Z. George agree that the main goal of the CIA should be to predict disasters? Why or why not?

Chapter 4

1. Marc A. Thiessen refers to "interrogation with enhanced techniques" rather than to torture. Based on the viewpoint

by Jeffrey Addicott, how might Thiessen justify his avoidance of using the word *torture*? How would it affect Thiessen's argument, if at all, if he were to use *torture*?

2. Imagine that you knew for sure that torture was an effective means of gathering intelligence. Why might it still be wise to avoid torturing suspects from an intelligence standpoint? Consider especially the viewpoints by George Friedman, Asha Rangappa, Matthew Alexander, and Larry Cox in crafting your answer.

Organizations to Contact

The editors have compiled the following list of organizations concerned with the issues debated in this book. The descriptions are derived from materials provided by the organizations. All have publications or information available for interested readers. The list was compiled on the date of publication of the present volume; the information provided here may change. Be aware that many organizations take several weeks or longer to respond to inquiries, so allow as much time as possible.

American Civil Liberties Union (ACLU)
125 Broad St., 18th Fl.
New York, NY 10004-2400
(212) 549-2500
e-mail: aclu@aclu.org
website: www.aclu.org

The American Civil Liberties Union is a national organization that works to defend Americans' civil rights guaranteed by the U.S. Constitution, arguing that measures to protect national security should not compromise fundamental civil liberties. The ACLU publishes and distributes policy statements, pamphlets, and press releases with titles such as "In Defense of Freedom in a Time of Crisis" and "New National Security Strategy Misses the Mark."

Center for Defense Information
1779 Massachusetts Ave. NW, Ste. 615
Washington, DC 20036
(202) 332-0600
fax: (202) 462-4559
e-mail: info@cdi.org
website: www.cdi.org

The Center for Defense Information is a nonpartisan, nonprofit organization that researches all aspects of global security. It seeks to educate the public and policy makers about issues such as weapons systems, security policy, and defense budgeting. It publishes the monthly *Defense Monitor* and the study "Homeland Security: A Competitive Strategies Approach."

Center for Security Policy (CSP)

1920 L St. NW, Ste. 210
Washington, DC 20036
(202) 835-9077
e-mail: info@centerforsecuritypolicy.org
website: www.centerforsecuritypolicy.org

The CSP is a nonprofit organization that informs the debate and ensures effective action on vital national security issues. The CSP believes America should have a strong national defense and should promote security through military, economic, and diplomatic means. The organization's website details several CSP projects relating to terrorism, Middle East policy, energy security, and national defense. The website also includes daily national security briefs and papers such as "Are You Safer? The Center for Security Policy Reports on the Obama Administration."

Central Intelligence Agency (CIA)

Office of Public Affairs
Washington, DC 20505
(703) 482-0623
fax: (703) 482-1739
website: www.cia.gov

The CIA was created in 1947 with the signing of the National Security Act (NSA) by then-president Harry S. Truman. The NSA charged the director of central intelligence (DCI) with coordinating the nation's intelligence activities and correlating, evaluating, and disseminating intelligence that affects national security. The CIA is an independent agency, responsible to the president through the DCI, and accountable to the American people through the Intelligence Oversight Committee of the U.S. Congress. Publications include *The World Factbook, World Leaders*, and numerous monographs and papers.

Council on Foreign Relations

58 E. Sixty-eighth St.
New York, NY 10021
(212) 434-9400
fax: (212) 434-9800
website: www.cfr.org

The council specializes in foreign affairs and studies the international aspects of American political and economic policies and problems. Its journal *Foreign Affairs*, published five times a year, includes analyses of current conflicts around the world. Its website publishes editorials, interviews, and articles, including The Roundtable Series on the Role of the Private Sector in Homeland Security and "Strengthening the Nuclear Nonproliferation Regime."

Federal Bureau of Investigation (FBI)

935 Pennsylvania Ave. NW, Rm. 7972
Washington, DC 20535
(202) 324-3000
website: www.fbi.gov

The FBI, the principal investigative arm of the U.S. Department of Justice, has the authority and responsibility to investigate specific crimes assigned to it. The mission of the FBI is to uphold the law through the investigation of violations of federal criminal law; to protect the United States from foreign intelligence and terrorist activities; to provide leadership and law enforcement assistance to federal, state, local, and international agencies; and to perform these responsibilities in a manner that is responsive to the needs of the public and is faithful to the Constitution of the United States. Press releases, congressional statements, and major speeches on issues concerning the FBI are available on the agency's website.

National Security Agency (NSA)

9800 Savage Rd.
Ft. Meade, MD 20755-6248

(301) 688-6524
website: www.nsa.gov

The National Security Agency coordinates, directs, and performs activities such as designing cipher systems, which protect American information systems, and producing foreign intelligence information. It is the largest employer of mathematicians in the United States and also hires the nation's best codemakers and codebreakers. Speeches, briefings, congressional testimonies, and reports are available on the NSA website, including such titles as "Counterinsurgency in Pakistan," and "Views About Armed Contractors in Operation Iraqi Freedom."

Rand Corporation

1776 Main St., PO Box 2138
Santa Monica, CA 90407-2138
(310) 393-0411
fax: (310) 393-4818
website: www.rand.org

The Rand Corporation is a nonprofit institution that helps improve policy and decision making through research and analysis. The corporation has studied terrorism for thirty years and has published numerous books on that subject as well as on foreign policy and national security. Research papers on these topics are also available on the its website.

Reason Foundation

3415 S. Sepulveda Blvd., Ste. 400
Los Angeles, CA 90034
(310) 391-2245
fax: (310) 391-4395
website: www.reason.org

The libertarian Reason Foundation promotes individual freedoms and free-market principles and opposes U.S. intervention in foreign affairs. Its publications include the monthly *Reason* magazine, recent issues of which are available at www.

reason.com. The foundation's website, linked to the Reason Public Policy Institute at www.rppi.org, publishes online versions of institute articles and reports, including such titles as "Big Brother Bush Is Watching, Listening, and Buying Info About You," and "Obama's Neverending Afghan Adventure."

U.S. Department of Homeland Security (DHS)
Washington, DC 20528
(202) 282-8000
website: www.dhs.gov

Created just after the September 11, 2001, terrorist attacks, the DHS was envisioned as a central agency that could coordinate federal, state, and local resources to prevent or respond to threats to the American homeland. The DHS contains many subdivisions that deal specifically with trade, immigration, preparedness, and research. The DHS website contains speeches and Congressional testimony by DHS representatives, as well as mission statements and departmental performance records.

Bibliography of Books

Michael Chertoff   *Homeland Security: Assessing the First Five Years.* Philadelphia, PA: University of Pennsylvania Press, 2009.

Anthony H. Cordesman   *The Lessons of Afghanistan: War Fighting, Intelligence, and Force Transformation.* Washington, DC: Center for Strategic and International Studies, 2002.

Allen W. Dulles   *The Craft of Intelligence: America's Legendary Spy Master on the Fundamentals of Intelligence Gathering for a Free World.* Guilford, CT: Lyons Press, 2006.

Douglas F. Garthoff   *Directors of Central Intelligence as Leaders of the U.S. Intelligence Community, 1946–2005,* rev. ed. Washington, DC: Potomac Books, 2007.

Jennifer K. Harbury   *Truth, Torture, and the American Way: The History and Consequences of U.S. Involvement in Torture.* Boston, MA: Beacon Press, 2005.

Henry M. Holden   *FBI 100 Years: An Unofficial History.* Minneapolis, MN: Zenith Press, 2008.

Robert Jervis   *Why Intelligence Fails: Lessons from the Iranian Revolution and the Iraq War*. Ithaca, NY: Cornell University Press, 2010.

Loch K. Johnson   *The Oxford Handbook of National Security Intelligence*. New York: Oxford University Press, 2010.

William R. Johnson   *Thwarting Enemies at Home and Abroad: How to Be a Counterintelligence Officer*. Washington, DC: Georgetown University Press, 2009.

Mark M. Lowenthal   *Intelligence: From Secrets to Policy*. Washington, DC: CQ Press, 2009.

Alfred McCoy   *A Question of Torture: CIA Interrogation from the Cold War to the War on Terror*. New York: Owl Books, 2006.

David L. Perry   *Partly Cloudy: Ethics in War, Espionage, Covert Action, and Interrogation*. Plymouth, UK: Scarecrow Press, 2009.

Ahmed Rashid   *Descent into Chaos: The United States and the Failure of Nation Building in Pakistan, Afghanistan, and Central Asia*. New York: Viking, 2008.

Jeffrey T.
Richelson

The US Intelligence Community, 5th ed. Boulder, CO: Westview Press, 2007.

Sam C. Sarkesian, John Allen Williams and Stephen J. Cimbala

US National Security: Policymakers, Processes and Politics, 4th ed. Boulder, CO: Lynne Rienner Publishers, 2007.

Jennifer E. Sims and Burton Gerber

Transforming U.S. Intelligence. Washington, DC: Georgetown University Press, 2005.

Jennifer E. Sims and Burton Gerber, eds.

Vaults, Mirrors, and Masks: Rediscovering U.S. Counterintelligence. Washington, DC: Georgetown University Press, 2009.

Marc A. Thiessen

Courting Disaster: How the CIA Kept America Safe and How Barack Obama Is Inviting the Next Attack. Washington, DC: Regnery Publishing, 2010.

Gregory F. Treverton

Intelligence for an Age of Terror. New York: Cambridge University Press, 2009.

Paul Viotti, Michael Opheim, and Nicholas Bowen, eds.
Terrorism and Homeland Security: Thinking Strategically About Policy. Boca Raton, FL: CRC Press, 2008.

Seth Weinberger
Restoring the Balance: War Powers in an Age of Terror. Santa Barbara, CA: ABC-CLIO, 2009.

Tim Weiner
Legacy of Ashes: The History of the CIA. New York: Random House, 2008.

Jonathan R. White
Terrorism and Homeland Security: An Introduction. Belmont, CA: Wadsworth Cengage Learning, 2006.

Richard White and Kevin Collins
The United States Department of Homeland Security: An Overview. Boston, MA: Pearson Custom Publishing, 2006.

John Yoo
The Powers of War and Peace: The Constitution and Foreign Affairs After 9/11. Chicago, IL: University of Chicago Press, 2005.

Index